HARRINGTON- A SCREENPLAY

Written by

Gary W. O'Brien

Inspired by True Events

INT. BBC TELEVISION STUDIO, LONDON - FALL, 1949, EVENING

The INTERVIEWER is seated at her desk waiting for GEORGE
ORWELL to arrive. Behind her is a poster of Big Brother, the
bottom of which reads "1984". Big Brother has a heavy black
moustache and handsome features. Orwell, forty-six years old,
wearing a sports jacket with open collar, enters and sits
down. He is coughing. The TELEVISION DIRECTOR, unseen, is in
the Control Room.

                    INTERVIEWER
          Good evening, Mr. Orwell.

                    ORWELL
          Good evening. Sorry I'm late.

                    TELEVISION DIRECTOR (V.O.)
          OK. Starting the interview shortly.
          Are we all good? George, thanks for
          coming in. I know you're not
          feeling too chipper. This will be
          mostly for archival purposes, but
          we'll be using some clips here and
          there. Remember, if you wish to go
          deeper into a point, by all means.
          We'll not cut you off. We're only
          taping. This isn't live.

                    ORWELL
          My doctor says I shouldn't, but I
          need to smoke. Do you mind?

Orwell, bored, lights up a cigarette.

                    ORWELL (CONT'D)
          Ok. Better. How long did you say
          this was going to be?

                    TELEVISION DIRECTOR (V.O.)
          Maybe an hour. But as you prefer.
          We are good to go as long or short
          as you want.

                    ORWELL
          Understood. I'll stay on point so
          we shouldn't be too long. Hopefully
          my bloody cough will quiet down.
          Damn irritating. Seems to be
          getting worse.

                    TELEVISION DIRECTOR (V.O.)
          We're ready. Show time in 5, 4, 3,
          2, 1.

                    INTERVIEWER
We are here tonight with the
celebrated author George Orwell who
has just published a rather
frightening novel called *1984*. Mr.
Orwell, can you tell us what this
world of *1984* looks like?

                    ORWELL
Well, as I've said in other
interviews, in *1984*, there is no
real law or constitution to offer
protection. The State does what it
wants. Political opposition is not
allowed since independent thinking
is not allowed. There are no
objective truths, no standards like
the past by which to judge the
present. The Party is everything.
The Individual nothing.

                    INTERVIEWER
Before we get into your characters
Winston Smith, Julia and O'Brien, I
am curious as to why the setting is
a place called Oceania. Why have
you called it "Oceania"? People
have said they wish you could have
included some narrative on where
you came up with this word.

                    ORWELL
Well, as for the word "Oceania", I
think it must have come from some
buried memory, probably an old book
that is no longer read.

                    INTERVIEWER
Come, Mr. Orwell. Is it only a
coincidence that your "Oceania" is
a dystopia, while the book no one
reads any more, called *Oceana*,
though spelled slightly different,
is a utopia?

Orwell's interest is piqued.

                    ORWELL
Oceana? The book published in the
seventeenth century? By, by …

                    INTERVIEWER
          I think you know very well, Mr.
          Orwell. The name of the author is
          James Harrington.

Orwell pauses.

                    ORWELL
          There is no evidence of my using
          Harrington's *Oceana* as a model for
          my book.

Interviewer picks up a copy of *1984* and starts skimming.

                    INTERVIEWER
          Oh, but Mr. Orwell, you left so
          many clues! The Chestnut Café, for
          example, where the discredited
          leaders of the rebellion would
          gather. Does it not remind us of
          the Nonsuch Tavern where the
          Commonwealthmen used to meet? Then
          there are the purges of those who
          opposed the new regime. Sound
          familiar with what happened after
          the Restoration? And what about
          putting those arrested in the
          Ministry of Love, substitute the
          Tower of London, without a trial?
          My God, you even mention Oliver
          Cromwell and make a reference to
          "kissing the Pope's toe." Were
          these just flashes from some hidden
          memory, or were you not giving us a
          negative reminder of the original
          Oceana?

Orwell reflects.

                    ORWELL
          I had hoped, but never thought, my
          audience would pick up on these.
          I've always said the best books are
          those that tell what you already
          know. Hardly anyone knows about
          Harrington. *Oceana* has been
          swallowed up over the centuries by
          power struggles and war.

                    INTERVIEWR
          But what precisely were you trying
          to say about Harrington? That he
          was a failed prophet?
                    (MORE)

                    INTERVIEWR (CONT'D)
          That his vision of the common good
          was not possible?

                    ORWELL
          No! I have fought against
          totalitarianism my whole life. I
          once wrote a poem we live in an age
          where it is forbidden to dream.
          Harrington dreamt. He longed to
          bring humanity hope. He meant to be
          the political author of the modern
          world. Instead, like my Winston, he
          became its heretic. Writers seldom
          admit to all their sources of
          inspiration. We want to keep our
          readers guessing. But if you really
          want to know why I chose the name
          of the novel's setting, it was to
          help us better appreciate
          Harrington's *Oceana*, which I admit
          is not the easiest book to get
          through. If the world had listened
          to James Harrington, even the
          contemplation of a world like *1984*
          would not be possible.

                    INTERVIEWER
          Perhaps you can tell us what you
          know about him. The Director said
          we are good to go as long as you
          want. Who was James Harrington, Mr.
          Orwell?

Orwell, very interested, his cough now under control, lights
up another cigarette.

                    ORWELL
          I don't know all his life. Just
          some highlights. Basically, he was
          a civilized man in an uncivilized
          world, who spoke truth to power. I
          am not sure if I properly
          interpreted the age we live in, but
          there is no doubt Harrington
          interpreted his….

Orwell begins to tell Harrington's story.

EXT. ROME, 1636, CARNIVAL PAGEANT, SHROVETIDE - MORNING

JAMES HARRINGTON and HENRY NEVILLE are strolling down a path
looking at various displays. Harrington stops at a kitchen
where the cooks are all trained cats.

Through the use of restraints, one cat turns a spit, another bastes the meat, another removes foam when the stock boils, and a fourth stirs green sauce. Harrington is twenty-five years old, well dressed, and speaks with a Lincolnshire accent. He is strong with thick, curly hair and a moustache. His eyes are hazel. Neville is seventeen. Handsome and clean-shaven, he is holding a book, Machiavelli's *Istorie Fiorentine*.

> NEVILLE
> James, it is Machiavel whom we
> might not but study. The Florentine
> is imploring us to look to facts,
> not ideals. Why are you stopping?
> We shall be late for the joust.

> HARRINGTON
> Oh, the depth of God's wisdom!
> Look, Henry.

> NEVILLE
> Pray, what is it? What do you see?

> HARRINGTON
> This kitchen where the cooks are
> kitlings. Regard! They have been so
> ordered the poor creatures can make
> no motion but to perform their
> proper function. Machiavel harps
> much upon a string he hath not
> perfectly tuned. He has seen the
> new world but not seen it well.
> Good orders can make us...

Suddenly, a YOUNG GIRL of about five years old who has been standing close to the cat kitchen, looks around and in panic starts to scream.

> YOUNG GIRL
> Mutter! Mutter!

Harrington speaks in Italian to her.

> HARRINGTON
> Tesoro, cosa c'è che non va? Perché
> stai piangendo? (*Sweetheart - what
> is wrong? Why are you crying?*)

The girl looks at Harrington without comprehension. THE OWNER OF THE CAT KITCHEN, who has also heard her scream, speaks in Italian to Harrington.

                    OWNER OF THE CAT KITCHEN
          Mi scusi signore. Viene qui tutti i
          giorni a guardare i gatti. Ho
          provato a parlarle ma lei non sa
          cosa le viene detto. (*Excuse me,
          Sir. She comes here everyday to
          look at the cats. I have tried
          talking to her but she knows not
          what is said.*)

                    NEVILLE
          "Mutter"? That is the German
          tongue.

Harrington speaks in German.

                    HARRINGTON
          Kind, warum weinst du? Wo ist Ihre
          Familie? (*Child, why are you
          crying? Where is your family?*)

                    YOUNG GIRL
          Ich kann meine Mutter nicht finden.
          Sie war dort und bettelte um den
          Baum. Sie ist verschwunden. (*I
          cannot find my mother. She was over
          there, begging at the tree. She has
          disappeared.*)

                    HARRINGTON
          Lass uns gehen und sie finden. (*Let
          us then go find her.*)

Harrington takes the girl by her hand and walks in the
direction of the tree. Neville follows. Suddenly the MOTHER
OF YOUNG GIRL appears.

                    MOTHER OF YOUNG GIRL
          Was machst du mit meiner Tochter?
          Nimm jetzt deine Hände von ihr! Ich
          war nur eine Minute weg. (*What are
          you doing with my daughter? Take
          your hands off her now! I was gone
          but a minute.*)

                    HARRINGTON
          Aber Fauline. Sie konnte dich nicht
          finden. Aber jetzt bist du hier.
          Ich meinte nicht krank. Darf ich
          fragen, was Sie in Rom machen? Sie
          sind weit von Ihrem Land
          entfernt.(*But Fauline. She could
          not find you. And now you are here.
          I meant no ill.*
                    (MORE)

HARRINGTON (CONT'D)
*May I ask what are you doing in
Rome? You are far from your
country.*)

MOTHER OF YOUNG GIRL
Das geht dich nichts an! Aber seit
Sie fragen, haben mein Mann und ich
vor sechs Monaten unser bayerisches
Dorf verlassen, um hierher nach Rom
zu fahren. Er war Künstler. Er
dachte, er könnte hier seinen
Lebensunterhalt verdienen. Aber vor
einem Monat wurde er in Florenz von
der Pest heimgesucht. Sein Tod kam
so plötzlich. Ich und meine Tochter
setzten unseren Weg hierher fort
und jetzt bin ich gezwungen zu
betteln. Sie amüsiert sich jeden
Tag, indem sie die Katzen in den
Käfigen dort drüben beobachtet (*It
is none of your business! But since
you ask, my husband and I left our
village in Bavaria six months ago
to make our way to Rome. He was an
artist. He thought he could make a
good living here. About a month ago
in Florence he was struck by the
plague. His death came so suddenly.
I and my daughter continued our way
here and now I am forced to beg.
She amuses herself every day by
watching the cats over there.*)

HARRINGTON
Wo wohnst du, Fauline? (*Where are
you staying, Fauline?*)

MOTHER OF YOUNG GIRL
Auf der Strasse. Wir haben wenig
Geld. (*On the street. We have
little money.*)

HARRINGTON
Nein. Das geht nicht. Geh zu meinem
Gasthaus. Es heißt Campo de Fiori.
Es ist dort drüben, ein
zwanzigminütiger Spaziergang. Sag
ihnen, dass du mein Gast bist. Mein
Name ist James Harrington, der
Engländer. Frag sie Für ein gutes
Zimmer für Sie und Ihre Tochter.
Ich werde heute Abend zurückkehren.
(MORE)

HARRINGTON (CONT'D)
In der Zwischenzeit ist hier eine
Lira, die Ihnen durch den Tag hilft
(*No. This will not do. Go to my
inn. It is called the Campo de
Fiori. It is over there, a twenty-
minute walk. Tell them you are my
guest. My name is James Harrington,
the Englishman. Ask them for a good
room for you and your daughter. I
will return tonight. In the
meantime, here is some lira to help
you through the day.*)

MOTHER OF YOUNG GIRL
Gut, in Ordnung. Aber es wird kein
Dankeschön geben. Fass meine
Tochter nie wieder an. Wenn Sie das
tun, werde ich die Poliziotti
anrufen (*Well, alright. But there
shall be no thank you. Never touch
my daughter again. If you do, I
shall call the poliziotti.*)

Harrington and Neville start walking away.

NEVILLE
Decent, Harrington. But why throw
your bounty away on such an
ungrateful person?

Harrington smiles.

HARRINGTON
Growing up in Lincolnshire, from
which I hail, there was much
famine. We learned early the
importance of helping he who
wanteth bread. I try to teach my
younger sister we must never be
mercenaries, selling our gifts to
expect so great a return as
gratitude. What I preach, I might
not but follow. Allow us make
haste, Henry. A joust awaits!

EXT. ROME, PIAZZA NAVONA - SAME MORNING

Harrington and Neville are sitting in the public stands
waiting for the start of the Saracen Joust, part of the
Shrovetide Carnival festivities. Jousters from four gates
will gallop their horses and lance the Saracen, an armour-
plated dummy. The competition will be won by the knight who
hits the Saracen's shield and obtains the highest score.

                          NEVILLE
          James! These Catholics are not so
          ill. They enjoy to party ere their
          priests turn them to stone during
          Lent! Allow us be Catholics today!

                          HARRINGTON
          One would think Rome is once more
          being overrun by Goths and Vandals.
          Italians, in their sports, are more
          extravagant than the wildest!

Neville stands up and speaks in Italian.

                          NEVILLE
          Signore! Vino! Vino! Possiamo avere
          una bottiglia qui? Assicurati che
          sia la migliore bottiglia che hai!
          (*Sir. Wine! Wine! Can we have a
          bottle over here? Make sure it is
          the best bottle you have!*)

The wine-seller brings a bottle and Neville pays him. The
jousters enter the arena and the competition begins. Neville,
still standing, looks around the crowd and sees a large,
beautiful woman.

                          NEVILLE (CONT'D)
          That lady has no weapon, James, but
          it will take a Goliath to fit her
          scabbard. He shall need at least
          six fingers to feel her!

Harrington laughs.

                          HARRINGTON
          Our tutor warned me your blood was
          hot. Try not to let it sear you,
          Henry.

Neville sits down, opens the bottle, and shares it with
James.

                          NEVILLE
          Now Harrington, at dinner last
          night, you discoursed about getting
          an invitation to see the Pope. What
          is all that about?

HARRINGTON
I am meeting him this afternoon. Our Ambassador to Venice has arranged for me to attend Candlemass, the blessing of the candles. His Holiness wishes to talk with someone having family connections to the King. You are welcome to join along.

NEVILLE
We met yet last night so I know not your history. You have connections to the English Crown?

HARRINGTON
We share a common lineage with the Stuarts.

NEVILLE
And art thou married?

HARRINGTON
No, yet one day perhaps. At this time, reading, learning, and touring Europe are my focus. But I did leave someone back home. A clever girl named Anne.

NEVILLE
And your plans, Sir, when you return?

HARRINGTON
Manage my dead father's estates since I am the eldest son. And continue to study and write. But whom can imagine the days ahead? The English monarchy has a dangerous flaw which many aim to gnaw. There may be war. And what of your future, young friend?

NEVILLE
Providence did not make me the eldest son, James. Wherein Father died, 'twere my older brother who inherited all, leaving me nought, just my wit to compose my fortune. I have an idea but one too early to act upon. The laws of this old gothic castle what be England are so unfair, so scandalous.
(MORE)

NEVILLE (CONT'D)
Why should the eldest son be a King
or another the sole inheritor of
his father's riches?

HARRINGTON
I always have felt the plight of
younger children is like that of
puppies. We take one, lay it in the
lap, feed it with every good bit,
and drown the other five. But you,
Neville, join as well from a
distinguished family, do you not?
Is there not a rumour 'twere your
grandfather whom wrote the Bard of
Avon's plays?

NEVILLE
Aye. Our family talks of that.
Grandfather, the Sir Henry Neville,
knew him of course. Many of his
plays were set in cities the Bard
had ne'er visited. Grandfather knew
'em. Padua, Venice. He was our
Ambassador to France. The man left
no proof so we shall never know.
Still I hope his talent for
composing, would he had any, hath
fallen my way. When I finish at
Oxford, I intend to write.

HARRINGTON
And what shall you write about?

NEVILLE
Of things I am passionate, but with
humour and satire. They may be
libelous. Actually, I have two
stories in mind. The first about a
sailor named George Pine who is
shipwrecked on a desert island with
four females. Left on their own,
they engage in free sexual tryings.
By the time Pine dies, he has
fathered almost fifty issue. They
then procreate. And after that, a
third generation. Wherein the
island gets finally discovered,
there are hundreds and hundreds of
Pines. But a civil war hath started
and the island is in chaos.

HARRINGTON
And what shall you call this novel?

                    NEVILLE
"The Isle of Pines".

                    HARRINGTON
Perhaps it be better called "The
Naughty Pines". Or "The Isle of
Penis". My God, if this is your
first book, I hate to imagine a
second.

                    NEVILLE
Another satire I call "The
Parliament of Ladies". It will be
about how the well-affected women
in England decide to summon a
Parliament of their own after the
legal Parliament - made up of men
of course, as is England's way -
has adopted a law saying every man
can have two wives. The women
debate how unjust this law is. They
feel instead of men having two
wives, every woman should'st have
two husbands. They will say:
"wasn't every woman born with two
legs, two hands, two eyes, two
ears? Doesn't a deep well have two
buckets? One for coming up and one
for going down? Marriage must be
like a bow which has two strings.
If one breaks, the other holds". Do
you follow?

Harrington laughs.

                    HARRINGTON
Exactly. While one goes off the
hooks, the other stays on its
hinges.

                    NEVILLE
That is it!

                    HARRINGTON
Does not every tavern have a front
door and a back door? Does not
every city have at least two gates?
Every bed two posts the better to
support the other parts of them?

                    NEVILLE
Enough. Enough. Methinks you have
it.

                    HARRINGTON
          Perhaps add an explanation like
          this. A preamble of sorts: "Whereas
          maids for the most part marry in
          haste and repent at leisure..."

                    NEVILLE
          Perhaps, my older friend, you
          should write it.

Harrington laughs.

                    HARRINGTON
          No, no! I shall not have a finger
          in that pudding. Much too saucy for
          me. But my Anne would join such a
          Parliament. Any other plans?

                    NEVILLE
          Actually yes. To have a seat in the
          real House of Commons. Grandfather
          served there and I wish to follow.
          And you, James? Do you not consider
          presenting yourself as a candidate
          some day? There cannot be a more
          noble profession.

                    HARRINGTON
          Being "in" Parliament will ne'r be
          for me, Henry. Better "without".
          There is not any public person,
          especially not any magistrate or
          legislator, who has written about
          politics worth a button. New
          visions are bid for but they
          require study. Wherein we return
          home, allow us keep in touch. We
          may collaborate on how to
          relinquish England's rotten
          foundations and erect new ones.

                    NEVILLE
          A grand imagining, James
          Harrington. It shall be an honour
          to join you.

INT. ST. PETER'S BASILICA, PAPAL ALTAR - THAT AFTERNOON

THE EARL OF DENBIGH, Basil Feilding, is standing to the side
of the altar. He is twenty-six years old, tall and bulky,
with a thick neck and a course, brutal face. He wears copper
framed spectacles and is constantly resettling them on his
nose. Harrington and Neville arrive.

                    HARRINGTON
          Lord Denbigh, please greet my new
          friend, Henry Neville. We shared
          the same tutor at Oxford. He has
          paused his studies for a short
          visit to Rome, as seems to be the
          fashion. Thank you again for
          arranging this.

                    DENBIGH
          Nice to meet you, Mr. Neville.
          'Twere no easy matter, James.
          Protestants are not usually
          welcomed here, especially English
          ones. Still business is business.
          The Pope knows you have family
          connections with Charles and is
          hungry for information about
          England. After Urban begins the
          mass, form a line with the other
          pilgrims and introduce yourself. He
          shall talk to you there. Mr.
          Neville, you and I shall await
          hither.

                    NEVILLE
          Good luck, James. For me, I would
          rather read Cicero than talk to
          this Pope. Granted how he treated
          Galileo, the man can only be a
          paranoid and a criminal.

                    HARRINGTON
          Urban's real sin is to foreswear
          liberty of conscience. Till we had
          Christianity, there ne'r were wars
          of religion. Europe must rid itself
          of its priestcraft. Yet my
          conversation shall be friendly.
          Allow us hope he is not crossed to
          reasonable debate. I shall try not
          to offend.

POPE URBAN VIII enters and begins the Candlemass ceremony,
conducted in Latin. He is sixty-seven years old, refined with
aristocratic bearing, and an excellent speaker. He knows
English.

                    URBAN VIII
          Auxilium nostrum in nomine Domini.
          (*Our help is in the name of the
          Lord*).

> ALL
> Qui fecit cælum et terram. (*Who made heaven and earth*).

> URBAN VIII
> Dominus vobiscum. (*The Lord be with you*).

> ALL
> Et clamor meus ad te. (*May He also be with you*).

> URBAN VIII
> Dominus vobiscum. (*Let us pray*). Dominus Jesus Christus, Filius Dei vivi, benedicat has candelas ad nostram petitionem humilibus consentientes. Ut digneris eos Dominus ex virtute crucis sancti…
> (*Lord Jesus Christ, Son of the living God, bless these candles at our lowly request. Endow them, Lord, by the power of the holy cross…*)

Harrington has joined the line of pilgrims and waits to be received by the Pope. When the prayer is finished, Urban blesses candles with incense. He distributes them to the clergy while the choir sings a canticle.

The Pope greets each pilgrim. A clergy assistant offers a candle which they take, bow down, and kiss the Pope's feet. It is now Harrington's turn. He speaks to the Pope in Latin.

> HARRINGTON
> Pater sancte, et gratias ago, quia non sum licet mihi in occursum adventus tui. James ex Anglia nomen meum Harrington. Non est in nostra Legatus imponeret ad urbem deportandos, Domine Denbigh, interius, quod ego huc ad meam tibi maxima respectu: Sancti Patris.
> (*Holy Father, I am so grateful you have allowed me to meet you. My name is James Harrington from England. It is through our Ambassador to Venice, Lord Denbigh, that I am here to give my greatest respect to you, Holy Father*).

> URBAN VIII
> 'Tis enough Latin for now. Oh yes, Mr. Harrington. I remember.
> (MORE)

URBAN VIII (CONT'D)
Denbigh asked if I could meet you.
We have but a few minutes. So, Mr.
Harrington from England, who are
you?

HARRINGTON
My lineage is drawn from the blood
of our monarchs. The Harringtons
were close to the Tudors and now
the Stuarts. King James made my
great uncle guardian of his
daughter Elizabeth. He saw to her
education.

URBAN VIII
James, that vulgar buffoon! Tell
me, Mr. Harrington, is it true
James told once your uncle not to
teach Elizabeth the classics since
Latin had the way of making women
more cunning? The man was an ass.

HARRINGTON
His son would not dispute with you
his father's character.

URBAN VIII
And what of Charles? He seems the
frailest of the Renaissance
monarchs. I am told his interests
are hunting and playing tennis
while the people plan to take his
government off its hinges. It is
said his favourite psalm is number
fifty-five - "Be merciful unto me,
O God, for man goeth to devour me."
Pray, Mr. Harrington, how did his
government come to be so decayed?

HARRINGTON
Holy Father, I have had the honour
to meet King Charles. In his heart,
he is a good man, yet poorly
advised. Be assured he wants no
Catholic blood spilt during his
reign. But you are right. England
is tottering on a cliff and daggers
are drawn. The only reason why the
people of England will blow up
their King is their King did not
first blow them up. We must
configure new covenants to keep us
from anarchy and corruption.

                    URBAN VIII
Yet covenants, Mr. Harrington, are
ne'r a sufficient check on
government. Authority comes from
God and all temporal power is
secondary to the spiritual. I ne'r
oppose good decrees yet subjects
might not but have a sense of good
moral character. The Church is the
only earthly force to lead the way.

                    HARRINGTON
Your Holiness, as the Florentine
hath written, "the voice of the
people is the voice of God." The
people may not see, but they can
feel. We need to trust in the laws
and orders they make.

                    URBAN VIII
Our time is short. Say to me about
your Protestant divines who bid
themselves "Puritans". I hear their
wish is to prepare for the return
of the Son of God. They forebear
not from quoting the Bible. Doth
they not understand religion cannot
be used line by line? The book of
Isaiah had something to say about
this.

                    HARRINGTON
I recall the verse, Holy Father.
Isaiah, number twenty-three. "So
then, the word of the Lord to them
will become/ Do this, do that/ A
little here, a little there/So that
as they go, they will fall
backward/ They will be injured and
snared and captured."

                    URBAN VIII
Just so, Mr. Harrington. You know
thy Scripture. Surely England must
see the falsehoods of such leaders
and the infectious itch of their
scribbling politicians.

                    HARRINGTON
I wish I could tell you they do,
yet such be not the case. A civil
war may join which our ancient
constitution, which is no
constitution, canst not forebear.
                    (MORE)

                    HARRINGTON (CONT'D)
          My aim is to study the reasons for
          strengths and weaknesses in
          governments. I intend to find a new
          politics, based on principles from
          which first premises are made, a
          science as rational as mathematics,
          with history as its guide.

                    URBAN VIII
          Youth hath so much ambition but by
          old age it most oft lies broken
          towards the floor. I know something
          about politics, Mr. Harrington.
          During this long war Europe is
          fighting, the weight of Christendom
          lies on my shoulders. Believe me.
          Palpable politics can ne'r be a
          science. There are no first
          propositions, only circumstances.
          Politics is an art which changes
          not from one era to the next. It
          has never been about honour but
          rather, with God's blessing,
          stopping those that threaten you –
          men like Galileo – and building
          alliances. Knowing thy friends and
          thy enemies, though they may seem
          like friends. Take Denbigh over
          there. Charles appointed him his
          Ambassador, which should'st hast
          made him a friend. When I size the
          man up, it is clear to me Denbigh
          would betray his King in a wit. He
          would forswear anyone if 'twere to
          his advantage. Allow me a word of
          advice. The work of a philosopher
          is safe whilst you stay in your
          library. But if thou enter the
          politics, keep thy guard. Those
          with power are rarely friendly or
          forgiving.

While Harrington and the Pope are talking, Denbigh and
Neville, standing to the side of the altar, quietly chat.

                    DENBIGH
          You know, Neville, I admire King
          Charles, but privately, I wary of
          his Catholic Queen and her French
          counsellors. And now we have that
          popish loving Laud as Archbishop of
          Canterbury. It seems the Powder
          Plot may have succeeded after all.
                    (MORE)

                    DENBIGH (CONT'D)
If Charles be not careful, popery
shall return to England within five
years.

                    NEVILLE
Did you hear this story,
Ambassador? An important member of
the House of Lords was dying, and
for his perpetual wish would he
asked to see King Charles and
Archbishop Laud. The peer had
granted them such loyal office
throughout his lifetime they felt
they had no choice yet to attend
him. Within hours they arrived.
The Lord asked them to sit quietly
on either side of his bed and bore
each of their hands. Finally,
Archbishop Laud asked: "why didst
thy lordship bid us hither?" The
nobleman replied with his eyes
closing: "Jesus died 'twixt two
thieves. Mine only hope is to try
the like."

                    DENBIGH
Good one. That pleasantry shall
last forever. Say to me, Neville.
Do you know what kind of fun Urban
VIII hath? Nun.

                    NEVILLE
That too shall last.

Neville and Denbigh laugh. Suddenly, they look to the altar
where there is a commotion. The Pontifical Swiss Guard has
been summoned. They take Harrington by the arm and escort him
from the altar and out the Cathedral. Denbigh and Neville
join him outside.

                    DENBIGH
Harrington. God, man. Pray, what
hath happened?

                    HARRINGTON
Things were going well. Our
conversation courtly and pleasant.
Then the pontiff was laying into
you most unfairly about how you are
not be trusted. My audience was
suddenly at an end. The priest
standing beside me offered a candle
as a souvenir of my visit which I
took.
                    (MORE)

                    HARRINGTON (CONT'D)
          He then said I could now kiss the
          Pope's toe. I looked at Urban and
          said: "Since I had had the honour
          to kiss His Majesty King Charles'
          hand, it was beneath me to kiss any
          other prince's foot." He grabbed
          the candle back and called the
          Guard. I fear I have set back
          relations 'twixt London and Rome.

Harrington, Denbigh and Neville leave laughing.

INT. BBC TELEVISION STUDIO, LONDON - SAME EVENING

The interview with Orwell continues. He smokes.

                    ORWELL
          Well, after that indelicate
          diplomacy, Harrington left Rome to
          study in Venice. Given that Europe,
          with its Kings and Dukes, was
          overwhelmed in a bloody Thirty
          Years War, Harrington was taken by
          Venice's democratic and stable
          institutions. He felt the city was
          designed by God to be a republic.
          He stayed there four years. When he
          returned home, England was on the
          verge of a civil war. What caused
          it is a debate which lasts till
          this day. Mismanagement by the
          King, a struggle for the rights of
          Parliament, religious ferment from
          "Puritans" and those calling
          themselves "The Fifth Monarchists".
          Harrington had his own ideas but
          was reluctant to get involved. Yet
          all that changed when he was
          dragged into it. For a while, the
          advantage lay with the King. Then
          came the Battle of Naseby.

EXT. ROYALIST CAMP, SOUTHWEST ENGLAND - JUNE 14, 1645,
MIDNIGHT

EDWARD HYDE, Lord Chancellor of England, thirty-six years
old, is waiting for news about the Battle of Naseby which
took place earlier that day. Civilians and soldiers are
lounging by an open fire, eating and drinking.

                    A SOLDIER
        Lord Chancellor, how much longer
        must we wait till we receive
        tidings? It does eat us up.

                    HYDE
        We'll get news soon. We are but two
        hundred miles from Naseby.

                    A SECOND SOLDIER
        How didst we get into such a mess,
        Mr. Hyde? Pray, what be your
        thoughts?

                    HYDE
        That is easy. This war is simply
        the result of men's wickedness –
        the pride of this man, the
        popularity of that – and the
        spouting of slogans by Parliament.
        They are nought yet but a pack of
        knaves and villains. The King can
        ne'r abide doing their bidding.

                    A CIVILIAN
        Yet what of the King, Mr. Hyde?
        Does Charles not share some of the
        blame for starting this war and
        letting it hie on and on?

                    HYDE
        From the beginning, the royal cause
        has been a shipwreck. The King,
        though brave, doth not trust
        himself and listens to those who
        are inferior to him. And fortune
        hath not been on his side. At
        Nottingham when he raised his
        standard, against my advice, he
        planted it towards the common for
        all to see, instead of inside the
        castle's walls. But then the rain
        came and blew it into the mud. The
        herald tried to read the King's
        declaration but it could not be
        done as the rain blotched the ink.
        A comical omen to begin our
        national tragedy.

Suddenly, a horse is heard galloping toward the camp. The men
rise, swords drawn. THE EARL OF CARNWATH, thirty-four years
old, exhausted and out of breath, dismounts.

HYDE (CONT'D)
Carnwath! I can only guess thou
rode directly from Naseby. Quick,
take the Earl's horse and get him a
brandy bowl. My Lord, what hath
befell at Naseby?

Carnwath, who speaks with a Scottish accent, tries to catch
his breath. He takes a drink of brandy.

CARNWATH
Thank you, Lord Chancellor. The day
was terrible. The King's army was
outnumbered nearly two to one. The
broil began well enough. Three of
Cromwell's regiments broke and
started fleeing. Ireton, his
deputy, was wounded in the brow and
taken prisoner. For a while it
looked, with God's blessed hand, we
might win. But then the
Parliamentarians' second line
started assaulting our left flank
and we were surrounded on three
sides. We had to retreat. At the
last minute our hardy but brainsick
King tried to launch a counter
attack. I had to seize his bridle.
I bid him: "Tolla-Thon. Ass hole.
Would thou go upon thy death in an
instant?" I didst not crave this
ungodly rebellion end in such a
futile gesture.

HYDE
'Tis so like Charles.

CARNWATH
Today is a day of infamy. O'er a
thousand men, mostly from our side,
are laying dead or dying at Naseby.
Many surrendered while others - the
Irish volunteers - were murdered
towards the spot. But the worst was
Parliament's cruelty to the Welsh
women who had followed their
officer husbands to cook and tend
their wounds. In chasing them down
the road to Farndon Field, those
pigs of Cromwell hacked to death
over a hundred and scotched the
faces of others. They bid them
whores, screamed they were witches,
and stole the money they had.
(MORE)

                    CARNWATH (CONT'D)
          How any one could support that
          bastard Cromwell after this causes
          meself vomit.

Carnwath spits. Hyde softly speaks.

                    HYDE
          Naseby was the battle of all for
          all, and we have lost it. Our fight
          is done.

Carnwath takes Hyde aside.

                    CARNWATH
          After seeing the King was made
          safe, I rode here directly to
          deliver two messages. One is a
          letter to his son. It is meant for
          his eyes only.

                    HYDE
          The Prince is sound asleep in the
          tent next to mine. The boy is only
          fifteen and I shall not wake him.
          This matter must be urgent, and if
          so, as Lord Chancellor, I need to
          know. Open it, Lord Carnwath, and
          read.

                    CARNWATH
          "My recent misfortunes remember me
          to command you that which I hope
          you will never have to obey. It is
          this. If I should at any time be
          taken prisoner, I command you never
          to yield to any conditions that are
          dishonourable upon any
          considerations whatsoever, though
          it were for saving my life. Your
          constancy will make me die
          cheerfully, praising God for giving
          me so gallant a son."

                    HYDE
          I shall convey it on the morrow.
          And the second message?

                    CARNWATH
          It is to thee, Ned. The King says
          there is now no probability but of
          his wrack. He desires thou to seek
          no treaties with Parliament.
                    (MORE)

                         CARNWATH (CONT'D)
          Wherein there is danger of his
          falling into rebel hands, he
          decrees you to take the Prince out
          of England and convey yourselves to
          France so he be with his mother. He
          hests you be the Prince's constant
          advisor, never leaving his side
          till his Throne is restored.

                         HYDE
          I shall obey. Allow me swear an
          oath that when his son returns, we
          will bring to punishment these
          bloody Commonwealthmen. Nay law or
          constitution shall forebear us from
          having our revenge.

INT. FLEET STREET, LONDON - LATER THAT YEAR

The Lock and Key is the shop, home and church of Pastor
PRAISEGOD BAREBONES. Barebones, a wealthy leather seller, is
forty-seven years old. He is with MR. GREENE, somewhat
younger, waiting to begin their church service.

                         BAREBONES
          Pastor Greene, for a conventicle,
          this is becoming a rather large
          gathering.

                         GREENE
          They are not all ours, Mr.
          Barebones. This congregation
          numbers not more than one hundred
          souls but there are many more than
          that hither. People are awaiting
          outside thy shop to get in and a
          crowd is filling all of Fleet
          Street. I even saw the Constabulary
          there.

                         BAREBONES
          Of no import. We might but ne'r
          shriek from the chance to speak
          God's true words. I am anxious to
          start. Begin the introduction.

                         GREENE
          Welcome old friends and granted the
          faces I am looking at, new ones as
          well. Welcome all to the Lock and
          Key, the home and shop of our
          Pastor, the well-liked leather
          merchant, Praisegod Barebones.
                         (MORE)

                    GREENE (CONT'D)
          We meet hither far aroint from the
          authority of the Church of
          England's bishops whom poison God's
          word with their Book of Common
          Prayer and their papist forms of
          worship. We shall find God
          ourselves! (Crowd shouts "Here,
          Here") And Pastor Barebones shall
          guide us! ("Here, Here") Mr.
          Barebones, the word is yours.

                    BAREBONES
          Dear friends, all of England groans
          under the tyranny of this King. The
          Bible tells us our last days shall
          be terrible. Doth thou not perceive
          the gouts of blood that hast fallen
          already - first at Edgehill, then
          Marston Moor, and now in the fields
          at Naseby? Yet Christ is at hand to
          draw up his glorious standard.

Barebones holds up a Bible.

                    BAREBONES (CONT'D)
          Friends, the history of man hath
          consisted of four Beasts - the
          empires of Babylon, then Persia,
          then Greece, and then Rome. The
          Good Book tells us the last Beast
          shall have ten horns and a little
          horn, which shall destroy the ten.
          After the fall of the last Beast,
          the Kingdom will be granted to
          Saints whom shall prepare for the
          second coming of Christ. And Christ
          and the Saints shall become the
          Fifth Monarchy whom shall reign for
          a thousand years.

Shouts of "Hurray! Christ will soon return!"

                    BAREBONES (CONT'D)
          Much is spoken of the rightful heir
          of the Crown and the injustice of
          casting him out. But, my friends,
          Jesus in the only right heir. We
          might not but confound this King
          and his bishops. Who can be against
          us if God in heaven is for us?

Shouts of "Leave our bishops alone!" Others yell "Leave us
be. Let us worship in peace!"

                    BAREBONES (CONT'D)
Dear friends, we must rise up and
bind this King in fetters. We
support the victories of Oliver
Cromwell whom shall change our
corrupted ways into a saintly
kingdom. Only he can set up a godly
republic. Cromwell is our new
Moses. He shall bring God's
vengeance on that tyrant Charles
and the Antichrist Pope.

As Barebones is finishing, there is great commotion as more
people attempt to get into the shop. Shouts are heard - "Down
with Cromwell! Long live the King!" "Stop this swarm of
separatists." Suddenly the mob smashes the windows. Members
of the congregation try to escape by going to the roof.
Fights begin and some are kicked while lying down. The
Constabulary enter and make arrests.

                    GREENE
Mr. Barebones, we had better rise
hither now. This crowd shall wreck
thy shop and burn it down.

                    BAREBONES
It shall take more than a mob to
stop us. We will have our revenge
upon the ungodly and anyone else
who crosses the Fifth Monarchy.
Fine, Mr. Greene, we might not but
depart. I know a way out. I think
not Jesus shall be coming back
today.

INT. BIRDCAGE WALK, CITY OF WESTMINSTER, LONDON - TWO YEARS
LATER, JANUARY, MORNING

The residence of James Harrington is a versatile timber house
on Birdcage Walk, a street named after the Royal Menagerie
and Aviary located there. LADY ASHTON is Harrington's younger
sister. She is married to a leading Member of the House of
Commons, General Ralph Ashton. Harrington is thirty-six years
old, his sister six years younger.

                    LADY ASHTON
James. It is I. Where are you,
darling brother?

                    HARRINGTON
Elizabeth, my dear Lady Ashton.
Whither else but in my library.
                    (MORE)

                    HARRINGTON (CONT'D)
          All by yourself, sister? Where's
          the General? Where's Ralph?

Lady Ashton enters Harrington's library.

                    LADY ASHTON
          My much-wearied husband returned
          north this morrow. There is
          constituency business in Lancashire
          needing attention. Ralph said
          Parliament has tidings of which you
          must know. But let that wait. How
          is my big brother coping with our
          country split down the middle
          because of religion and politics?

Harrington, who has been smoking, puts down his pipe.

                    HARRINGTON
          Straddling the centre, safe from
          harm's way. Yet not idle, dear
          sister. Wherein I am not back in
          Rand, I spend my time in here.

                    LADY ASHTON
          Such books! In Greek, Latin,
          French, and Italian. And all the
          ancient masters. You have been
          blessed, James. God has given you
          the natural inclination for study,
          to speak foreign languages, and to
          write. Growing up, your desire for
          knowledge rather frightened Mother
          and Father.

                    HARRINGTON
          I am happy here, Elizabeth. A man's
          study is his garden which furnishes
          a variety of flowers. I mimic
          Machiavel who, on entering his
          library, clears the mud from his
          apparel, and for the next many
          hours feeds towards the food of
          ancient men, forgetting every pain.
          Look, I am making translations of
          the Roman poet Virgil. I dabble in
          poetry myself, writing love-verses.
          But Neville tells me to forebear
          such tampering since my muse is
          rough.

                    LADY ASHTON
          Writing love verses? Not for Anne
          Darrell, be they? Canst you read me
          one?

                    HARRINGTON
          All right, sister, yet it may be
          painful to the ear. And yes. I
          admit it is for Anne.

Harrington reads from a page.

                    HARRINGTON (CONT'D)
          "I never flatter'd Prince nor will
          I thee/Yet things and persons,
          well distinguished and loved,
          we/What is possible, and what is
          not may see."

                    LADY ASHTON
          Hardly sweet talk, James. Henry may
          be right. Restrain this pining!
          Anne is gone, living in Paris.
          Enjoying life, drinking wine, and
          taking this new thing bid "snuff"
          which be all the rage. She has her
          own money and depends on no one. I
          still receive letters from her. We
          had such fun back in Rand, when we
          were children. I miss her.

                    HARRINGTON
          As I do, sister. Yet I fear my
          longing Anne Darrell shall last
          forever. What tidings do you bring?

                    LADY ASHTON
          Since the King's surrender to the
          Scots at Newcastle, negotiations
          have dragged six months. The Scots
          have lost all patience. They will
          be handing the King to us at
          Holdenby House over in
          Northamptonshire. Ralph wants you
          to know last night Parliament
          appointed a commission to take
          charge of the King. It will be
          headed by the Earl of Denbigh. You
          know him, James. He was Ambassador
          to Venice before the war - you were
          with him in Rome.

HARRINGTON
Denbigh? His appointment is
prudent. Wherein the war broke out,
he was the only one of his issue to
range himself with Parliament. At
the battle of Edgehill, he led a
regiment against his own father. I
hear he now regrets his ingratitude
toward the King. I would him well.

LADY ASHTON
Yet there is more. Denbigh is on
his way hither. Parliament wants
you to accompany the delegation and
be a servant to the King, to be
part of his court officials, and
assist them in their negotiations.

HARRINGTON
Me? Why?

LADY ASHTON
Ralph feels it is because thou art
well thought of by Parliament,
despite the fact you engage not
with any faction. Though we have
family connections to the Stuarts,
they regard you as a generous
friend. They hope you might gain
the King's trust.

HARRINGTON
I am not involved, Elizabeth. I am
only James of Sapcote sitting safe
in his library, translating Virgil,
and but speculating what kind of
government can deliver England from
its plight.

Lady Ashton hears a carriage coming and goes to a window.

LADY ASHTON
Your Stoic life is at an end,
James. You must descend the cloud
you are sitting on and hand
Virgil's wisdom a new task. Bring
your learning of the ancients to
Holdenby House. Fate has drawn you
into history. Look, there is
Denbigh's carriage.

EXT. OUTSIDE HARRINGTON'S RESIDENCE - A FEW MINUTES LATER

Harrington and Lady Ashton go onto the street and talk to
Denbigh through the window of his carriage. Denbigh adjusts
his spectacles.

                    DENBIGH
          Good morrow, Lady Ashton, and to
          thee James. I like your house. Not
          far from Parliament or the coffee
          clubs. I have not been on Birdcage
          Walk for some time. Wherein I was
          studying at Cambridge and came to
          London, I would walk over here to
          see the King's Menagerie. There
          were aye a lot of strange
          creatures. I remember particularly
          this one bird or animal, ne'r sure
          'twere. Seemed like some sort of
          waterfowl, a cross 'twixt a stork
          and swan.

                    HARRINGTON
          It's bid a pelican, Basil. 'Twere
          granted to the King by the Russian
          Ambassador. It can toss up and turn
          a flounder and get it right into
          his guillet. I oft walk there
          myself just to see this creature.

                    DENBIGH
          Lady Ashton, I met your husband
          last night in the Lords library and
          he told me you might be dropping by
          to see your brother. I guess you
          have informed James about the job
          Parliament hath granted us.

                    LADY ASHTON
          Yes, Basil. A commission to entreat
          the King at Holmby.

                    DENBIGH
          Me and a pack of others. Two more
          from the Lords and six from the
          Commons. As well, there will be so-
          called "private gentlemen" to wait
          about the King as his servants.
          These the King might not but
          approve of. Harrington, they want
          you to be one of his private
          gentlemen. Naseby hath inflicted a
          blow the King shall ne'r recover
          from.
                    (MORE)

DENBIGH (CONT'D)
Yet he refuses to accept any
demands from our side. He's still
hoping for popular uprisings or
help from his royal cousins in
France or Spain. He wants a second
civil war and by God, we might not
but forebear it!

HARRINGTON
You were so kind to me in Rome and
Venice, Basil. Of course, I accept.
Though I am unsure in my own mind
what a Parliamentary victory over
Charles shall look like. Any new
government hath got to be a union
the interests of the whole nation,
not private ones, housed by
covenants and meet procedures.

DENBIGH
Never start playing utopian games
with me, James Harrington. Now be
not the time. People are not
interested in thy theories of
history or the glories of the
government of Venice. This is a
time for real discourse - for
practical politics. The King lives
in a dream world of feudal times,
which hast now passed. You live in
a future orb of justice and
liberty. Want we to get thou and
the King focused on the world of
actual life!

LADY ASHTON
But Basil, you know, I know, my
husband knows, and the women of
this country know, that if this
King is done away with and we are
left with those malignants like
Cromwell and his religious
fanatics, wither England under that
sort of republic? If the desire be
to leave feudalism and embrace
modernity, my brother is the best
one to guide you. James wants to
build a new Parliament where every
stone is squared in the quarries of
ancient prudence. It will prove a
Bethel, a house of the divine, and
not a Babel, a tower of confusion.
(MORE)

                    LADY ASHTON (CONT'D)
          The corner stones will neither
          recline, decline or incline but
          stare straight up to heaven and be
          fixed upon a foundation of naked
          truth.

Denbigh pauses.

                    DENBIGH
          Well, alright then. Haply, James,
          thou shall be of more help than
          Parliament even knows. We ride
          together to Holdenby House in my
          carriage. Pack well and I shall
          join back towards the morrow. We
          could be gone for some months.

EXT. HOLDENBY HOUSE, NORTHAMPTONSHIRE - MORNING

Denbigh, the other Parliamentary Commissioners, the
Chaplains, and the LORD MAYOR OF HOLDENBY are standing at the
entrance of Holdenby House to await the arrival of the King.
In formation as well are the "private gentlemen", including
Harrington and THOMAS HERBERT, who will act as the King's
servants. Denbigh resettles his glasses.

                    DENBIGH
          Lord Mayor, everything in order?

                    LORD MAYOR OF HOLDENBY
          The village of Holbenby hath worked
          diligently, Earl Denbigh, to
          welcome our King. We, like everyone
          else, summon peace. We have
          assembled a household staff of over
          a hundred. His table will be served
          with almost thirty divers dishes
          each day. There are beautiful
          gardens to walk in. Hither at
          Holdenby House, King Charles shall
          hast all he desires.

                    DENBIGH
          My colleagues thank thee, Lord
          Mayor, for getting the House
          content so apace. Let us pray the
          King doth not become an
          insufferable guest.

KING CHARLES I arrives at Holdenby House, guarded by troops.
A short man, he is forty-six years old. Cheers go up from the
local townspeople. Denbigh bows to the King who gives him his
hand to kiss. Denbigh kisses it.

> DENBIGH (CONT'D)
> Your Highness, I trust thy trip
> from Newcastle, though long, was
> not unpleasant. On behalf of
> Parliament, I welcome you hither to
> Holdenby House with the sincere
> hope we can remove all distrusts
> and establish a right understanding
> betwixt you and Parliament.

> KING CHARLES
> I might not but thank Parliament
> for permitting me to flee the Scots
> but you paying four hundred
> thousand pounds to do so was too
> cheap a rate. Perhaps here at
> Holmby, I shall have the leisure to
> ponder questions and engage in
> pious exercise, something I have
> not tried these past five years. At
> least I have taken leave of my
> nagging wife.

Denbigh chuckles.

> KING CHARLES (CONT'D)
> Allow me look upon thee, Denbigh.
> So here you are - heading
> Parliament's commission to bring me
> to my senses. I thought so well of
> you when you took your place in
> Parliament I granted you that
> posting of Ambassador to Venice,
> the most sought-after position in
> all of England. And look how you
> rewarded me. Thy shame might not
> but haunt you - such betrayal of
> your King, as well as your father!
> He told me how you broke his heart
> at Edgehill. You fighting with the
> Roundheads and him loyal to his
> King, as his oath demanded. I wot
> thou wounded me. Hath one
> sovereign ever been betrayed by so
> many of his "loyal" subjects! Hath
> any age seen such deceit!

> DENBIGH
> Your Majesty, the infirmity in my
> heart for my actions are real. I
> told Hyde that at Uxbridge and I
> know thou knowest it.

                    KING CHARLES
          Alas, you are not alone in
          betraying me. The list is long -
          peers, members of the Commons, the
          army, the navy, so many Divines.
          Yet should'st I speak so
          innocently? I myself betrayed my
          chief minister, the Earl of
          Strafford, and signed the bill for
          his execution. Should'st Strafford
          have been impeached for his
          administrative failings? Perhaps.
          Yet executed at Tower Hill ere
          three hundred thousand people? I
          signed his death warrant to protect
          myself and my family. Strafford
          didst not deserve to die. I too am
          sick at heart.

                    DENBIGH
          The Bard of Avon who wrote those
          plays once said "what is done is
          done and cannot be undone." We
          might not but bear to this. We have
          a job to do here, and should our
          work be just, we can start a new
          beginning for our country.

                    KING CHARLES
          I agree, Lord Denbigh. God gave us
          eyes in the front of our head to
          look forward, not backward. We must
          try our best to settle the unhappy
          differences between us.

                    DENBIGH
          The Lord Mayor assures me you shall
          have all you desire hither.

The King turns to the Lord Mayor.

                    KING CHARLES
          Yes, thank you, Lord Mayor.
          Everything but my freedom.

                    DENBIGH
          I must remind Your Majesty that you
          are Parliament's prisoner.

                    KING CHARLES
          Prisoner, Sir? I am not an ordinary
          prisoner. I am still the King.

DENBIGH
Before His Majesty enters his new
quarters, let me introduce the
Chaplains who will assist you
spiritually. They are of the
Assembly of the Divines.

KING CHARLES
They are Presbyterian Chaplains, I
presume? Which means I will be
deprived of my Prayer Book? I must
say Denbigh, they are not here to
assist me in my duties to God but
rather to convert me to their form
of worship. There will be no
religious services here at
Holdenby. Thank you very much,
gentlemen, but I shall spend
Sundays in my room in study and
prayer.

DENBIGH
As Your Majesty wishes. Let me also
introduce to you the private
gentlemen who shall be attending
you as your court officials, if you
agree. They will provide for your
Majesty's well being and safety.

KING CHARLES
And no doubt, guard against my
escape.

Each gentleman bows as they are introduced.

DENBIGH
Sir Fulk Grevil, Knight.

KING CHARLES
How do you do, Sir Grevil.

DENBIGH
Mr. Anthony Mildman.

KING CHARLES
Good day, Mr. Mildman.

DENBIGH
Mr. Ansty.

KING CHARLES
Mr. Ansty.

                    DENBIGH
          Mr. Babington.

                    KING CHARLES
          Good day, Mr. Babington.

                    DENBIGH
          Mr. James Harrington.

                    KING CHARLES
          Mr. Harrington. And where did you
          study, Mr. Harrington?

                    HARRINGTON
          At Oxford, Your Majesty.

                    DENBIGH
          And finally, Mr. Thomas Herbert.

                    KING CHARLES
          Good day, Sir. Mr. Herbert, were
          you not in the cabinet of my
          Ambassador to Persia, Sir Dodmore
          Cotton?

                    HERBERT
          I was.

                    KING CHARLES
          I hear you are well travelled. I
          have also learned you are a strong
          supporter of Parliament. Perhaps
          you shall change thy mind once you
          get to know me.

Charles returns to Harrington.

                    KING CHARLES (CONT'D)
          Tell me, Lord Denbigh. Was it not a
          James Harrington you told me about
          some years ago that had an amusing
          rencontre with the Pope in Rome?

                    DENBIGH
          The very same, Your Majesty.

                    KING CHARLES
          Mr. Harrington, we have met before,
          have we not?

                    HARRINGTON
          Yes, Sire, at the wedding of your
          Chief Justice.

                    KING CHARLES
          Oh yes. Then I am honoured to meet
          you again, although the times are
          not quite so happy. My father spoke
          well of your great uncle, Baron
          Harrington of Exton. Now, Mr.
          Harrington, when Lord Denbigh was
          my Ambassador - after which he
          turned his back on me - he told me
          a story about you and Urban VIII at
          Candlemass when you refused to kiss
          the toe of that papist ass. Didst'
          thou not think kissing his feet
          might be viewed as a sign of
          respect to a temporal prince, one
          who has spiritual responsibilities
          as well, as have I?

                    HARRINGTON
          As I told the pontiff, since I had
          the honour to kiss Your Majesty's
          hand which I did, you may recall,
          at the wedding, I thought it
          beneath me to kiss any other
          prince's foot.

                    KING CHARLES
          Well done, Mr. Harrington! When
          Denbigh told me that story I
          laughed and laughed. I was so
          impressed by your loyal and witty
          reply. Your irreverence was
          priceless. I hope it brought that
          trouble-making Italian bastard a
          few pegs down in his closet.
          Denbigh, methinks for the instant I
          shall choose Mr. Harrington and Mr.
          Herbert to be the gentlemen
          admitted to my privy chamber. I am
          well satisfied with their sobriety
          and good education. I approve of
          these others and you can select
          yourself their duties.

                    DENBIGH
          Thank you, Your Highness.

The King and the welcoming party go into Holdenby House.

INT. GOVERNOR'S CASTLE, ISLE OF JERSEY - ONE WEEK LATER.

Hyde, still Lord Chancellor but now in exile, sits in the
Governor's library.

The Governor of the Jersey Isle is SIR GEORGE CARTERET. THE
SECRETARY TO THE LORD CHANCELLOR, an older, frail man,
enters.

                    SECRETARY TO THE LORD CHANCELLOR
          Lord Chancellor, the Governor of
          the Isle of Jersey, Sir George
          Carteret, to see you.

                    HYDE
          Good to see you, Carteret. We seem
          to be the only two officials still
          performing their offices on
          unconquered English soil. Praise be
          to God the Isle of Jersey hast yet
          been saved from the swine who wish
          to root up our monarchy.

                    CARTERET
          Good day, Lord Chancellor. Some
          tidings, Sir, yet they might be
          dated. I hast been privy the King
          is now at Holdenby House as a
          prisoner. He is no longer in
          custody of the Scots yet of
          Parliament. They hath appointed
          Lord Denbigh to be their chief
          negotiator. I thought you should
          know.

                    HYDE
          Thanks, George, yet I was aknown
          already. Although the Royalists are
          scattered, I have made sure the
          King's secret forces are still
          functioning. Rest assured I know
          exactly what is going on in
          Holdenby House. We have a man there
          and he ciphers me tidings daily. I
          doubt would they ever guess his
          identity. Even the King does not
          know. This civil war is not yet
          over. It hath simply entered a new
          phase. Negotiations. As aye, we
          shall employ the one remaining
          political good we have - time, and
          our man at Holdenby shall help us.
          Let us see who blinks first.
          Parliament is so divided. They need
          a settlement yet it must be on our
          terms, my terms really.

                    CARTERET
          And what kind of terms shall they
          be, may I bid?

                    HYDE
          The Tudors are long dead and so
          shall the Stuarts would they never
          adapt. We must build a new State,
          governed by a new class of men.
          This King, any King, might ne'r
          again be shackled by Parliaments.
          Look what that hath brought us. We
          might not but be allowed to do what
          is necessary to protect the State.
          The party, not written covenants,
          shall be in charge. The head of
          this State will be a support for
          his friends and the terror of his
          enemies. And anyone standing in our
          way shall be surprised. There can
          be no dissent and forsooth no real
          democracy. I shall personally see
          to that.

INT. LONDON, NONSUCH TAVERN, BOW STREET, COVENT GARDEN -
MORNING

Barebones and Greene are sitting at a table. Their serving
girl is MARY ELLIS, twenty years old, who attends the Sunday
services at the Lock and Key.

                    GREENE
          Mr. Barebones, I cannot tell you
          enough how glad I am we have
          resumed our conventicles. Our
          congregations are growing bigger
          each week.

                    BAREBONES
          Yes, Mr. Greene, it may be a sign
          Christ's kingdom is imminent. But
          we have got to do something other
          than merely preach. Ah, here is our
          serving girl now.

                    MARY ELLIS
          Good day, Gentlemen. Welcome to
          Nonsuch Tavern. What may I bring?

                    BAREBONES
          Methinks we would both welcome
          coffee, my dear.

                    MARY ELLIS
          Please by your leave, Pastor
          Barebones? I am Mary Ellis. I and
          all the other servants here hither
          to thy services at the Lock and Key
          every Sunday. We love your message
          Christ is King and He shall be anon
          returning. I read the Bible every
          night. Especially the book of
          Daniel.

                    BAREBONES
          Doth thou remember verse 44? "And
          in the days of these kings shall
          the God of heaven set up a kingdom,
          which shall never be destroyed."

                    MARY ELLIS
          "And it shall stand forever." Yes,
          of course. It is my favorite. What
          'ere could be a ranker dream than
          that. I listen when I bring our
          guests their drink and hear talk of
          so much bloodshed, so much sorrow.
          I myself am suffering - my brother
          was killed, fighting that false
          King at Naseby. Shall it be anon,
          Preacher, when our Lord Jesus
          returns?

                    BAREBONES
          Good daughter, if we do our duty
          and prepare His coming, many
          believe it shall be.

Mary's eyes shine.

                    MARY ELLIS
          That will be a day beyond what I
          e'en imagine. We might not but ne'r
          hie back to what we hast been. We
          must put a stop to the evil in this
          world. Thank you, Pastor, for
          everything you do. I shall get you
          gentlemen your coffee.

                    GREENE
          Judging by Miss Ellis hither, we
          may be finding support among young
          people.

                    BAREBONES
          Our message is growing, Mr. Greene,
          yes. But there is more to be done.
                    (MORE)

                    BAREBONES (CONT'D)
I personally know Thomas Harrison,
the lawyer-soldier who is a good
friend of Oliver's. I've talked to
Harrison many times. He too is a
believer in the Fifth Monarchy. He
agrees it is now time we be a
political force within this
country. It sits only on bayonets
and not much else. The so-called
"ancient constitution" is a filthy,
frog infested pond. Saintly men
must rule in a new kind of
Parliament, one unfettered by any
laws except the word of God. Thomas
flatters me when he says we shall
bid it "The Barebones Parliament".

                    GREENE
I am told the King hath been made a
prisoner at Holdenby House. He is
locked up with the Presbyterians
hoping they can get him to agree to
a settlement. Parliament hath e'en
brought in that philosopher, the
aristocratic Commonwealthman James
Harrington, who lives over on
Birdcage Walk, to persuade the King
to submit to Parliament's will.

                    BAREBONES
Yes, I know. Harrison is privy as
to what is going on at Holmby and
keeps me informed. I know
Harrington. He believes not that
government can be built on godly
principles. He comes into my shop
now and then and we debate. He
boasts he is a republican but loves
that bishop-loving King. He shall
only muddy the waters and be of no
aid to anyone. The army has no use
for the man.

                    GREENE
So, what should'st we be doing?

                    BAREBONES
Keep preparing for the New
Jerusalem. Harrison will continue
talking to Cromwell to get him to
hit together to a Parliament of
Saints. In the meantime, you and I
shall work hard to have this anti-
Christ of a King hanged.
                    (MORE)

                    BAREBONES (CONT'D)
          If we have to, we will use force to
          establish the rule of the godly.
          Methinks time - this time - shall
          be with us. The Lord will soon be
          revealing his wonderous plan.

INT. HOLDENBY HOUSE, KING'S BEDCHAMERS - FIVE MONTHS LATER,
EARLY JUNE MORNING

Charles is preparing for the day.

                    KING CHARLES
          Mr. Herbert, could thou please
          inform Lord Denbigh and the other
          Commissioners I shall not be
          discoursing with them today? I
          desire to take a walk over to
          Althorp. The Spencers have such a
          beautiful estate and I hast not yet
          paid the Earl a visit. 'Tis mine
          hope only Mr. Harrington accompany
          me. There are things arising from
          our common lineage about which I
          desire to discuss with him in
          private.

                    HERBERT
          I am sure the Commissioners would
          not object, Your Majesty, as long
          as I and the other gentlemen can be
          with you and Mr. Harrington at a
          distance, both in front and behind
          you.

                    KING CHARLES
          I warrant, Mr. Herbert, I shall not
          be attempting an escape today. Mr.
          Harrington, are thou content?

                    HARRINGTON
          I should like that, Your Majesty.

Charles takes his walking stick.

                    KING CHARLES
          Well then, let us make haste. I am
          quick and lively in my motions and
          anxious for exercise.

EXT. PATH FROM HOLBENBY HOUSE TO ALTHORP - SAME MORNING

Charles and Harrington start their walk to Althorp, two miles away.

                    KING CHARLES
          May I say, Mr. Harrington, I am
          glad Parliament has chosen you to
          serve me hither at Holmby. Yet
          though we have been together
          several weeks, I am afeared I do
          not know you well. Are you married,
          Mr. Harrington?

                    HARRINGTON
          Sadly, no, Your Majesty.

                    KING CHARLES
          Sadly, Mr. Harrington? Say to me a
          bit of thy story.

                    HARRINGTON
          It is an old story I am sure you
          heard before. I had a love - still
          do. We grew up together. Her issue
          also served the Stuarts. We changed
          eyes as children. Yet, unwisely, I
          left her to go on my Grand Tour and
          now she is gone. I never mind
          telling you, Your Majesty, in my
          heart, I am chained to Anne. At
          night those chains are heavy.

                    KING CHARLES
          Yours is a tender story and very
          close to my own. About twenty years
          since, I also unwisely went abroad -
          to Madrid, to find my bride. The
          King of Spain's daughter, the
          haunting Infanta Donna Maria. All
          the princes of the Continent were
          chasing her as well. My God, what
          an attractive woman. She had the
          finest hair and complexion, and the
          fairest hands. Yet the situation
          was hopeless. Attempting to get
          Catholic Spain to hit together to a
          marriage with a Protestant prince
          from England was like trying to get
          honey of the bee without the danger
          of being stung. My father thought I
          was a fool. I returned heartbroken
          and, 'twixt us, have remained so to
          this day.
                    (MORE)

                    KING CHARLES (CONT'D)
Despite my troubles with politics
and religion, it is the Infanta I
imagine every night before I drift
to sleep. Ay, Mr. Harrington,
love's chains can be most heavy.
Yet you are still young. Belike
Fate shall change its course.

                    HARRINGTON
It is true the ways of Providence
are inscrutable, for both you and
I, Your Majesty.

                    KING CHARLES
Now, Mr. Harrington, there is
something else I desire to ask. I
hast grown so tired of the
Cavaliers flattering me. Not my
wife of course. She is always
frank, despite her hatred of the
English language. She says it is
for my own good. But her candor
appears mostly as brutal and
unloving. I never welcome it. The
talk at Court, when I had a Court,
was would I canst not control my
wife, how may I expect to control
Parliament? They say we are now
living in a new, more modern age
and things shall ne'r be the like
again. I wonder whether that means
wives will forbear berating their
husbands? Do you think that will
change, Mr. Harrington, in this new
age we live?

                    HARRINGTON
Or shall men forebear beratting
their women? I doubt if either man
or woman's nature shall change,
whatever the era. The passions are
seldom easily controlled. But haply
if we can make wives, as well as
husbands, freer, they may be
happier. Perhaps this be a wistful
thought. We may be left with only
better laws and education.

                    KING CHARLES
As for Parliament, there is too
much hypocrisy. They are oft
affable, yet their disguise shall
ne'r enclave the fact they want to
make me a dead dog.
                    (MORE)

                    KING CHARLES (CONT'D)
They are like spiders who draw
poison from the most wholesome
plants. Mr. Harrington, I have
always found it difficult to make
friends. Prithee, what is your
assessment of me and my situation?
Now, hither in the tranquility of
Holdenby House, I hope you and I
can remove our masks.

                    HARRINGTON
Parliament knows I love Your
Majesty. I hast ne'r hidden this. I
showed it in Rome. But to flatter
is not my duty. Allow me declare
with all that is true you are
clearly a prince of great virtue
and piety. Thou hast clung to what
your father taught you about
dignity and conscience. You were
brave in battle at Naseby. Your
collection of paintings has helped
England present itself as a major
power. But there is more to this
collection than just diplomacy. One
day, England shall be grateful for
your affection of the arts.

                    KING CHARLES
And the negatives, Mr. Harrington?
What flaws in my character may hast
gotten us into this civil war?

                    HARRINGTON
Frankly, I do not think flaws in
character have much to try with
your predicament or England's. A
plant grows the worse for not
understanding the manner of its
vegetation. You believe Parliament
has broken the law and the judgment
of heaven is on your side. You are
certain that if you do not break
Parliament, Parliament will break
you. You fail to see your enemy is
the Presbyterian divines who stand
behind Parliament and urge it on.
They blame you for many sins - like
listening to Laud and not
themselves. Their aim is to abolish
the bishops root and branch, and
strip you of your powers. Yet these
are symptoms, not causes, Your
Majesty.

Charles stops walking and looks intently at Harrington.

                    HARRINGTON (CONT'D)
          I need to tell you, my King,
          something your councillors, like
          Edward Hyde, should have told you
          before, that England's form of
          government - monarchy - has a
          dangerous flaw in it and it is not
          in the power or wit of man to cure.

                    KING CHARLES
          And what flaw is that, Mr.
          Harrington?

                    HARRINGTON
          That government must be the empire
          of laws and not of men.

Charles resumes walking.

                    KING CHARLES
          Am I not a man? My ancestors and I
          have been making laws for
          centuries, and better ones than
          that House of lawyers and
          grammarians. This false bunch only
          seek to further their own
          interests. They are like tradesmen
          who knit nets, not make law.

                    HARRINGTON
          Your Majesty is right. All laws are
          made by men. But it is plain that
          where the law is made by one man,
          there it may be unmade by one man.
          As to why hath our country so
          broken apart, it is clear the
          origins lay in society itself. As
          is the balance of wealth, such is
          the nature of government. Power is
          determined by the distribution of
          property. When the people truly own
          the soil and the wealth - and where
          there is a balance amongst the
          people in that ownership - the
          government might not be democratic.
          There is an awakened gentry class
          demanding political power equal to
          their economic wealth. They do lack
          civil and religious liberty and
          believe sovereignty derives not
          from a divine power yet from the
          people.
                    (MORE)

HARRINGTON (CONT'D)
They desire to have a Commonwealth and they are not wrong.

KING CHARLES
Please Mr. Harrington. I do not endear to hear you speak of a Commonwealth. Such views are abhorrent to me. God has given me a duty to oppose any alteration of our government. It is but a watch which simply needs fine-tuning.

Harrington, his eyes on fire, grabs the King's walking stick and throws it down.

HARRINGTON
By Christ! Get it out of your mind government is simply a mechanical device which your Tudor ancestors hath handed to your father and you for safekeeping. That watch has broken and must be discarded for the time it reads is false. The age of feudalism is at its end. Your monarchy has fallen with such horror as hath been a spectacle of astonishment unto the whole earth!

Charles, taken aback, speaks quietly.

KING CHARLES
None hath spoken to me like that before. Not even my Generals in the depth of our despair. But I shall allow you to try so, Mr. Harrington. We are beyond the stage of polite words and niceties. I have told Parliament I am not crossed to reform.

Charles picks up his walking stick and continues on the path to Althorp.

KING CHARLES (CONT'D)
As my confident, what advice may you grant?

HARRINGTON
We must stop a second civil war and compose a peace. Instead of armies, let us use the weapons of our minds.

KING CHARLES

I welcome peace as much as anyone but I know not with whom I am negotiating. Is it the English or the Scots, or are they now together? And with whom in Parliament am I speaking? They are split betwixt the Calvinist Presbyterians who crave a reformed church, and the Independents who desire a complete separation of church and state. As for encroaching on my powers, the Presbyterians are fairly moderate though deep down they want to have me possess no more authority than a Duke in Venice which I will rather die than suffer. As for the Puritan radicals like Cromwell's New Model Army, they speak of me as "that man of blood." And it is they who are the rising power. It would not surprise me if the army purges Denbigh and his crew from Parliament and a Rump takes over demanding I be put upon the scaffold. Anything we agree to here at Holmby shall be broken. I distrust them as much as they distrust me. And they hate each other. Then there are those Bible-quoting fanatics the Fifth Monarchists who are also finding strength in Cromwell's army. These self-styled saints are the most dangerous threat of all. They think this is the time of the end and I am the last Beast mentioned in the Bible. They want me bound in chains and my head upon a gate. How doth I negotiate with that? In the meantime, my wife and son in Paris and my advisors like Ned Hyde think the royalist cause shall triumph once again. I am expecting Lord Lauderdale, the Scottish Commissioner, to be coming hither any day with a message from Hyde as to how myself should answer Parliament.

                    HARRINGTON
          Since you seek my advice, I would
          beseech Your Majesty not to meet
          Lauderdale. He is a canting
          hypocrite and any alliance with the
          Scots will only prolong this war.
          He and Hyde think they are "little
          kings" and bring but darkness. 'Tis
          they who crave to make thee a
          puppet. I told Denbigh a
          settlement with Parliament shall
          depend on moderation, particularly
          with regard to the established
          church. You are a good man and the
          meetest judge as to what needs to
          be done to stop this bloodshed. Do
          not let Hyde or Lauderdale confuse
          thee.

Charles stares at Harrington. He then unwinds.

                    KING CHARLES
          Well, we are hither. Lord Spencer's
          house is a fair one. Shall we rest
          awhile before paying our respects
          to the good Earl?

Harrington and the King sit down on some rocks overlooking
Spencer's vast estate.

                    HARRINGTON
          I need to smoke. Do you mind, Your
          Majesty?

                    KING CHARLES
          Not at all. Smoking was a regular
          habit at my Court and my father's,
          although he detested it. He once
          described smoking as "a custom
          loathsome to the eye, hateful to
          the nose, and dangerous to the
          lungs." Posterity may judge him
          right. Yet even he, with all his
          arrant power, could ne'r get that
          genie back in its bottle. The gold
          in America is not yellow but brown,
          as the farmers in Virginia and the
          Carolinas have discovered. Doth
          thou smoke often, Mr. Harrington?

                    HARRINGTON
          When in my library, yes. It seems
          to help me to better think. Would
          Your Majesty like to try my pipe?

                    KING CHARLES
          That had been nice, Mr. Harrington.
          I am not often tempted yet methinks
          now, in this place, is the right
          time.

Harrington and the King share the pipe. Suddenly, they see
someone on horseback galloping towards them.

                    KING CHARLES (CONT'D)
          Pray, who is he?

                    HARRINGTON
          It is Denbigh. This cannot be good.

                    DENBIGH
          Your Majesty, you must but return
          presently. We have just got word a
          Party of Horse is marching towards
          Holdenby. We know not as yet who is
          leading it. It may be Cromwell or
          at least one of the New Model
          Army's command, forsooth not
          Parliament's. I am told there are
          at least five hundred horsemen. I
          shall order the guard doubled and
          stand by, and not suffer any
          attempt upon your person. But the
          most I have is fifty men. It shall
          not be much of a fight. I fear
          this war has taken another turn,
          one which can only be for the
          worse. James, see to it the King
          gets safely back.

EXT. ENTRANCE TO HOLDENBY HOUSE - NEXT DAY, DAWN

A cavalry of horsemen approaches. They are led by CORNET
GEORGE JOYCE, thirty-one years old. Denbigh and the
Parliamentary Guards wait with swords drawn.

                    DENBIGH
          What doth thou desire?

                    JOYCE
          Say to the Guard to stand down,
          Denbigh. This can be no match.
          Besides they may desert you. We
          demand to see the King.

                    DENBIGH
          On whose authority? Who are you?

                    JOYCE
On my authority. I am commanding
this unit. I am Cornet George
Joyce.

                    DENBIGH
Soft, I know you. You were a
tailor's assistant in London ere
the war. You are only an Ensign,
the most junior rank of
commissioned officers. Often a
colonel had been heading a cavalry
command. Is this Cromwell's doing?
By God, Joyce! You are a Leveller
and an Agitator. What doth thou
desire with the King?

                    JOYCE
The army is tired of Charles Stuart
stringing this country along with a
carrot. Thou hast been hither at
Holmby five months trying to reach
a settlement. The army hath a new
humour and shall tolerate no more
fetches. This King shall account
for the blood he has shed. And I
shall be pleased to swing the axe.
Kings rule by consent and for the
good of the people. Should they
become tyrants, the people may
depose them. I am taking this
"King" to his just reward.

                    DENBIGH
You are doing a thing never yet
done on this earth. Stop this
madness.

Charles appears. He is dressed and prepared, having
anticipated he would be kidnapped. Harrington and Herbert
accompany him.

                    KING CHARLES
This commotion has awakened me but
I have been expecting it. Denbigh,
who are these troopers? What is
going on?

                    DENBIGH
This is Cornet George Joyce. Who he
is covering for he shall not say
but he and his horsemen have come
to remove you from Holdenby House.

                    KING CHARLES
          Mr. Joyce. What authority do you
          have to take charge of my person
          and carry me away?

                    JOYCE
          I am sent by the authority of the
          army to prevent the design of their
          enemies who seek to involve the
          Kingdom a second time in blood. I
          am acting in the name of the
          English people.

                    KING CHARLES
          That is no lawful authority. I know
          of none in England but mine, and
          after mine, that of Parliament.
          Have you a written commission?

                    JOYCE
          I have the authority of the army.

                    KING CHARLES
          That is no answer. I will ask
          again. Have you a written
          authority?

                    JOYCE
          I beseech Your Majesty to ask no
          more questions.

Joyce points to his troopers.

                    JOYCE (CONT'D)
          There is my commission behind me.

Charles smiles.

                    KING CHARLES
          I have never before read such a
          commission. But it is written in
          characters fair and legible enough.
          A company of as handsome proper
          gentlemen as I have seen in a long
          while. But to remove me hence you
          must use absolute force unless you
          give me satisfaction as to those
          just demands which I make. That I
          may be used with honour and
          respect. You are masters of my
          body. My soul is above your reach.

                    JOYCE
          If Your Majesty will enter the
          carriage. Enough talk. Let us begin
          our journey. We leave immediately.

Charles mounts the carriage and sits.

                    KING CHARLES
          For what place do you intend to
          take me?

                    JOYCE
          To the army headquarters at
          Newmarket.

                    HARRINGTON
          Wait, wait your Majesty. I must say
          goodbye.

Harrington approaches the carriage and kneels. Charles holds
out his hand and starts to draw Harrington in.

                    JOYCE
          Stop. Who are you?

                    DENBIGH
          He is James Harrington, a private
          gentleman appointed by Parliament
          to serve the King.

                    JOYCE
          I have known of you. You are the
          scholar. You have a reputation of
          being a learned republican yet our
          officers are offended by your
          defence of the King's false
          attitudes. Your attendance to
          Charles Stuart should have been
          dismissed weeks ago. All right,
          Harrington, you may enter the
          carriage to say farewell. Yet it
          shall be your final farewell. Do it
          with haste.

The King and Harrington talk inside the carriage.

                    HARRINGTON
          Who has granted Joyce his decrees
          do you think?

                    KING CHARLES
          Cromwell. Should I aye see him, I
          shall bid him but he will foreswear
          it of course.
                    (MORE)

                    KING CHARLES (CONT'D)
Lest he hangs up Joyce, I shall not
believe him. So, Mr. Harrington,
this is how it ends. I have been in
the custody of the Scots, then of
Parliament, and now of the army.
Unless I escape, this shall be my
last stop.

                    HARRINGTON
But surely Your Majesty, they will
continue to negotiate.

                    KING CHARLES
I used to think Parliament and the
army needed me more than I needed
them, yet that is no more. Oh, the
charade will last for a while. But
we all know the outcome, with me on
the scaffold. This is your modern
world, Mr. Harrington. Today the
lawns of Holdenby showed what that
world shall henceforth look like.
On one side me, representing the
law, however ill framed. Towards
the other side, Joyce with his
cavalry, which is as good a law as
can be executed by any judge in
England. In your new world,
governments shall try aught which
they regard is for the public
safety, "in the name of the
people", even breaking the law.
Neither I nor my father aye dreamt
of this. Going forward, the supreme
law will be "salus populi." And to
this all laws shall stoop. It shall
be the perfect handle for
demagogues to bear.

                    HARRINGTON
No. This shall not be. There must
be real protection against power.
And the greater the power, the more
danger of berattle. Nothing shall
justify breaking the law or the
constitution. With the right
orders, this sort of philosophy
will ne'r have a place in a modern
world.

                    KING CHARLES
Then see to it, Mr. Harrington. God
speed. Yet for now, adieu.
                    (MORE)

                    KING CHARLES (CONT'D)
          Ere what Cornet Joyce says, I pray
          I see you one last time.

Harrington is escorted from the carriage. He watches as
Charles, Joyce, and his horsemen leave.

EXT. LONDON, BANQUETING HOUSE, WHITEHALL PALACE - JANUARY 30,
1649, AFTERNOON

Crowds have gathered. A raised scaffold has been built into
the street and is draped in black with fences on the sides.
Access to the scaffold is from a taken-out window of
Banqueting Hall's first floor. Pikemen stand in front of the
scaffold. The day is clear and bitterly cold.

                    LADY ASHTON
          Hie, James. We are almost at
          Banqueting Hall. Prithee keep thy
          strength. At least this Rump of a
          Parliament is not killing the King
          in a corner. Belike they redeem
          themselves from that high handed
          and illegal trial.

                    HARRINGTON
          How uncivilized this new world has
          become. To behead a King! Is that
          Thomas Herbert near the stairs?
          Thomas, it is James. This is Lady
          Ashton, my sister. Is the King
          hither already?

                    HERBERT
          What a terrible time to be meeting
          you again, James. Hello, My Lady.
          Yes, Charles is here. He is in one
          of the rooms taking nourishment so
          he doth not faint. I was with him
          all last night. Unlike me, he slept
          quite well. He told me he doth not
          fear death and is prepared. The
          man's calmness overwhelms me. I was
          told to wait near the scaffold and
          then take care of the King's body.
          After he is interred, I am through
          serving this Rump.

Denbigh arrives.

                    DENBIGH
          Thomas. James. And Lady Ashton!

                    HARRINGTON
          Lord Denbigh!

                    DENBIGH
          I am going up. All the Ambassadors
          have been invited to witness this
          grotesqueness and as a former
          Ambassador, I qualify. I must move
          quickly. The King liked thou better
          than anyone at Holdenby, James.
          Doth thou would to join me?

                    LADY ASHTON
          Hie, James. I will stay with Mr.
          Herbert and we shall comfort each
          other. We shall be hither when it
          is over.

INT. BANQUETING HALL - MOMENTS LATER

The Hall is crowded with privileged visitors. Denbigh and
Harrington arrive just in time to see the King, accompanied
by a bishop, and guarded in front and rear, walking to the
window. As the King passes Denbigh and Harrington, he pauses.
He ignores Denbigh and speaks directly to Harrington.

                    KING CHARLES
          Is that you, Mr. Harrington? I fear
          my duty is now done. I do not think
          Hyde will be coming to rescue me,
          although judging by the number of
          soldiers, they think a royalist
          assay is possible.

While they are talking, the King's two Executioners, who are
disguised with masks and grey wigs, are also making their way
to the scaffold. They pass Harrington and the King. One of
them turns and whispers.

                    EXECUTIONER
          Gentlemen, this is as happy an
          occasion for me as it was at
          Holdenby House.

Charles gives him a penetrating look. He speaks quietly.

                    KING CHARLES
          So, Cornet Joyce. Why am I not
          surprised?

                    JOYCE
          Captain Joyce, Charles Stuart. I
          have since been promoted.
                    (MORE)

>JOYCE (CONT'D)
>I am here to complete your just
>sentence and send you to Hell.

>HARRINGTON
>You are doing Cromwell's bidding to
>the last. 'Tis is a job even
>London's Chief Headsman refused to
>try. Hide yourself well from
>history, Captain Joyce, the coward
>you are.

>KING CHARLES
>And enjoy the rest of thy day, Sir!

Joyce departs for the scaffold.

>KING CHARLES (CONT'D)
>What other surprises attend me? In
>fifteen minutes, I shall be finding
>out. Prithee join with me onto the
>scaffold, Mr. Harrington, while I
>meet eternity. In these
>circumstances, a loyal face is not
>unwelcome.

Charles speaks to the guards.

>KING CHARLES (CONT'D)
>Mr. Harrington shall be coming with
>me.

>GUARD
>No, he shall not.

>KING CHARLES
>In Christ's name he shall!
>Parliament is allowing other
>writers on to scaffold to record
>what is quoth. Mr. Harrington is a
>writer! I do lack mine own to
>ensure the record is true.

Guard reluctantly consents.

>GUARD
>All right. Parliament's cause has
>never been at odds with James of
>Sapcote.

EXT. EXECUTION SCAFFOLD - SECONDS LATER

Charles and Harrington walk on to the scaffold.

                    KING CHARLES
          Regard this howling crowd, Mr.
          Harrington. They want my head, not
          for what I hast done but simply
          because I am a threat to their new
          Commonwealth. Yet doth they even
          know what one is? They are forever
          enunciating principles but clueless
          as to their desires. Look at them!
          Presbyterians, Independents,
          Congregationalists, Anabaptists,
          Covenanters, Fifth Monarchists,
          Levellers, Diggers, Ranters, and
          Quakers. What a multi-head monster!
          All gathered hither to see the end
          of the English monarchy. This war
          hath undone the greatest work of
          time and cast this kingdom into a
          new mould. These are sobering
          times, Mr. Harrington, and I am a
          sober man. If anyone in England can
          discover them what a Commonwealth
          should'st be, it is you, James
          Harrington. Do this for me, for
          your country and for the ages. I
          might not but now say goodbye.

Charles reaches into his cloak.

                    KING CHARLES (CONT'D)
          Please take this small golden case
          as my legacy to you for the
          kindness and wisdom thou hast
          bestowed on me.

Harrington has tears in his eyes. He bows and kisses the
King's outstretched hand.

                    HARRINGTON
          Thank you, Sire. I and my family
          shall treasure it forever.

Charles whispers to the Executioner.

                    KING CHARLES
          Alright, Sir. 'Tis time to finish
          thy work.

Charles walks to the block, takes off his cloak, puts on his
skullcap and addresses the crowd.

                      KING CHARLES (CONT'D)
I shall be very little heard of
anybody here so I shall speak just
a word. I am a martyr to the people
and go from a corruptible to an
incorruptible crown, where no
disturbances can be in the world.

The King stoops down and lays his head upon the block.
Harrington watches in anguish as the King is executed. The
crowd is hushed and then groans and cheers after the axe
comes down. Joyce picks up the King's head. He says nothing.
Then a loud sound is heard as he throws the head down on the
planking. Now louder groans and cheers. Harrington can watch
no more. He breaks down and stumbles through Banqueting Hall
and out onto the street where Lady Ashton and Herbert are
waiting.

                      LADY ASHTON
James! What is happening to you?

                      HERBERT
Look. One side of his brow hath
drooped. Is his heart giving out?

Harrington can hardly speak.

                      HARRINGTON
It is not my heart although they
have just smashed it to pieces. My
face. I feel nothing.

                      LADY ASHTON
He is breaking down. 'Tis the shock
of this ungodly day. I shall take
him home and fetch a doctor. This
is his reward for assisting
Parliament. So much for this "Age
of Genius." Good luck to thee Mr.
Herbert, and God Save England. I
pity the gruesome office ahead of
you today.

She holds her brother in her arms and walks with him to find
a carriage.

INT. BBC TELEVISION STUDIO, LONDON - SAME EVENING

Orwell continues with Harrington's story.

                    INTERVIEWER
          You suggest Harrington went into
          shock after the King's execution.
          Did he recover?

                    ORWELL
          One writer who knew him said he
          contracted a disease from it,
          probably palsy, and for a long time
          had bouts of melancholy. It took
          him some years to recover, if he
          ever did. After the execution, he
          returned to his family estate at
          Rand, over in Lincolnshire, and
          dedicated himself to the study of
          civil government. In the meantime,
          Oliver Cromwell took power but was
          just one bloody disappointment,
          particularly to Harrington's
          friend, Henry Neville. One day,
          Neville paid James a visit.

EXT. RAND, LINCOLNSHIRE, HARRINGTON'S FAMILY ESTATE - SPRING,
1656, AFTERNOON

Harrington exits his house to greet a carriage carrying
Neville and his two nieces, CHARLOTTE and AMELIA. Harrington
is now forty-five years old, Neville thirty-seven. Charlotte
is seven and Amelia six. Also living at the Harrington estate
is the cook, JESSY.

                    HARRINGTON
          Henry! Welcome to Rand! I have been
          expecting you! So, what beautiful
          young ladies have you brought,
          Neville?

Neville and his nieces descend from their carriage. The girls
are giggling.

                    NEVILLE
          This is Charlotte and this is
          Amelia, my bother's daughters.
          Girls, this is my dearest friend,
          Mr. Harrington, who lives in this
          big manor hither at Rand. In
          earlier days, Mr. Harrington and I
          travelled to Italy.

                    HARRINGTON
          Do you ladies know where Italy is?

                    CHARLOTTE
          I do. On my father's map, it is
          shaped as a boot. Mr. Harrington,
          doth thou like riddles?

                    HARRINGTON
          Well, yes. I do, Charlotte.

                    AMELIA
          No, allow me to tell! What has to
          be broken before you can use it?

                    HARRINGTON
          Pray, I do not know, Amelia. Do you
          know Charlotte?

                    AMELIA
          Allow me to tell. An egg.

                    CHARLOTTE
          I know another yet let me answer it
          this time. Mr. Harrington, what
          makes an octopus laugh?

                    HARRINGTON
          That is difficult. What does make
          an octopus laugh, Charlotte?

                    CHARLOTTE
          Ten tickles. Dost thou understand,
          Mr. Harrington? Ten tickles.
          Tentacles. An octopus has tentacles
          yet very they are limbs.

                    AMELIA
          Do you know what an octopus looks
          like, Mr. Harrington? Like this!

Amelia, hunched over, starts waving her arms back and forth.

                    CHARLOTTE
          No, Mr. Harrington. An octopus
          moves this way!

Charlotte waves her arms up and down.

                    HARRINGTON
          Now ladies, you have proved to me
          you are both most, most smart, but
          also most, most silly. You deserve
          a reward. While your uncle and I
          talk, why not hie to the rope-swing
          tied to that big tree and play.
                    (MORE)

                    HARRINGTON (CONT'D)
          Jessy, my cook, shall bring you a
          nice cake. I imagine you are hungry
          after thy journey.

                    CHARLOTTE AND AMELIA
          Thank you, Mr. Harrington.

The girls depart laughing and, moving like octopi, go to the
rope-swing.

                    HARRINGTON
          Charming nieces, Henry. But no
          issue of your own? Thy wife still
          without affection? You rarely come
          to Rand. It has been months since
          we last spoke.

                    NEVILLE
          I regret to report my darling is
          still as cold as a Highland lake.
          Yet how could it be different? I
          married her when she was yet twelve
          years. She looks upon me more an
          uncle than husband.

                    HARRINGTON
          My dear Henry. Didst thou not
          regard there were ways of getting
          land and money other than marrying
          the underaged daughter and heir of
          a rich man recently died?

                    NEVILLE
          Please, James, no moral judgments.
          I told you in Rome about the plight
          of younger sons and how we must
          live by our wits. And 'twere not
          just I who thought up this scheme.
          Her mother was all for't. She
          wanted to make sure her husband's
          lands stayed out of the King's
          greedy hands. 'Twere she whom
          convinced her daughter marriage to
          me was the only thing to try before
          the King claimed wardship over her.
          'Tis called marriage politics. I
          am a politician. It is what I do.

                    HARRINGTON
          Yet thy wife puts up with you?

NEVILLE

It hath not all been ill. I am
wealthier than my father or brother
aye were. And at one time my wife
enjoyed the stories I read her ere
we bedded. She still laughs at my
rough ways and thinks it funny I
get beneath people's skins. But she
has declared I board her no more. I
ride at anchor now.

HARRINGTON

For sure thou hast got under
Cromwell's skin! He banned you from
London! He might have locked you in
the Tower for your pamphlet showing
his Protectorate nought yet a game
of cards made of knaves and
cheaters. How they dispatched "one
King and went for another." You
even made yourself a player who
proclaims ye shall not sit more
"for I am all day dreaming of
another game!" Thy grandfather
would have written more subtle.

NEVILLE

I fear Cromwell hath bettered us in
our game. James, what has happened
to our Commonwealth? Oliver is no
Protector! King Cromwell is but a
slippery politician who squashes
anyone who stands in his way. For
him, there is nought except plot
after plot. There is talk of giving
him the Crown. He came to power
dressed in ordinary clothes but now
has adopted the attire of a
monarch. How do we make the old
cause good once more? Sit in
libraries and compose translations
of Italian masters? Wallow in
melancholy and discontent?

HARRINGTON

There can be no more sheltering
from political storms. There is a
difference between having the sense
of the thing, and making the right
use of that sense. You must present
yourself as a candidate for
Parliament again, Henry. Carry high
thy grandfather's torch.
                    (MORE)

                    HARRINGTON (CONT'D)
As for me, I have recovered from my
sickness and now commit to both
talk and action. I am composing a
book. Well, more of a romance than
a treatise, much like Plato's *Laws*.
It will explain why Charles'
monarchy collapsed and lay down
principles that would enable a true
Commonwealth to function. The
details need working out - in fact,
I am at a puzzle of how Parliament
should work. I call my book *Oceana*,
the noblest land of the Northern
Ocean, an immortal Commonwealth!

                    NEVILLE
James, art thou sure you wish to
discourse publicly about an
imagined state? Oliver and his
bashaws, like Thurloe, will create
only danger for you, not to mention
the Royalists. Contemplating in a
library differs much from
pamphleteering.

                    HARRINGTON
A sober man once told me I've a
duty to set Cromwell and the people
of England aright. I can wait no
longer.

Jessy, Harrington's cook, interrupts their conversation.

                    JESSY
The cake be now ready, Mr.
Harrington.

                    HARRINGTON
Wonderful, Jessy. Allow us bring it
to Neville's charming ladies.

They walk to the rope-swing where the children are playing.

                    NEVILLE
Girls, say good day to Mr.
Harrington's cook, Jessy. She hath
made a cake for you both to share.

                    CHARLOTTE AND AMELIA
Good day, Jessy. Thank you, Jessy.

                    CHARLOTTE
May you cut the cake for us, Jessy?

                    JESSY
          Mr. Harrington, sir? Why not let
          the girls divide the cake? I found
          with mine own children 'tis a
          wonderful lesson that serves them
          well.

                    HARRINGTON
          A superb imagining, Jessy. Henry,
          let us see how thy girls share.

Jessy sets the cake down on a blanket and gives each girl a
fork. She hands a knife to Charlotte.

                    NEVILLE
          Hie ahead, Charlotte. Divide the
          cake.

                    AMELIA
          Yet Uncle, this is unfair.
          Charlotte shall surely take the
          better half. Grant me the knife.
          Since I am the younger, allow me
          divide and take the first piece.

                    CHARLOTTE
          That is not just either, Uncle.
          Amelia shall cut a larger piece and
          then eat it. Belike I should not
          divide the cake at all yet keep it
          myself. But that would not be fair
          to thee, sister.

Charlotte pauses to think.

                    CHARLOTTE (CONT'D)
          All right. I have an answer to this
          riddle. Amelia, you slice the cake,
          then I shall choose mine piece. Or
          let me divide, and you then choose.
          Such is the only way we both will
          be satisfied.

                    AMELIA
          That is fair. Charlotte, you divide
          and I will choose.

                    HARRINGTON
          Henry, are thou listening? "By the
          mouths of babes hath God set forth
          his strength!" This is the answer
          as to how to construct *Oceana's*
          Parliament.
                    (MORE)

                    HARRINGTON (CONT'D)
          That which philosophers are
          disputing upon in vain is brought
          to light by these two silly girls.
          The whole mystery of the
          Commonwealth lies in dividing and
          choosing. Such is how we arrive at
          the common interest. One House of
          Parliament shall have the natural
          right of dividing and the other of
          choosing. 'Tis so clear. A popular
          assembly without a second house
          will be not be wise and an upper
          house without a popular assembly
          will never be honest.

Neville thinks for a moment.

                    NEVILLE
          Yes, James, I see it. 'Tis equal
          that *Oceana*'s Parliament be two
          great assemblies, not one. A
          political fable must be written
          about how, if England were still a
          monarchy, some rude person will say
          to my two silly girls: "What,
          dividing and choosing? Who has
          taught you to cast away passion and
          interest when you make a decision?
          I will have no dividing. Give me
          all the cake." My girls shall then
          reply: "But who are you?" He would
          answer: "I am the King." And they
          would say: "By what right do you
          take our cake?" And he would reply:
          "By Divine Right!" Then he would
          snatch the cake away. In this
          Protectorate, Oliver acts no
          differently. By God, James. Finish
          Oceana and show the world what a
          true Commonwealth looks like!

INT. BIRDCAGE WALK, HARRINGTON'S LIBRARY - THAT FALL, MORNING

Harrington, smoking his pipe, sits at his desk looking at
papers. Lady Ashton rushes in. Harrington rises.

                    LADY ASHTON
          James! Bad tidings! Ralph just
          heard *Oceana* has been stopped at
          the printer. Cromwell's spymaster
          John Thurloe hath confiscated it.
          He sees it but as another plot.
                    (MORE)

> LADY ASHTON (CONT'D)
> Thurloe vows to be vigilant against
> any criticism of the Protectorate.

> HARRINGTON
> I thought I had been careful what
> be why I divided *Oceana* among three
> divers printers. A spaniel questing
> hath sprung my book out of one
> press into two others.

Lady Ashton pauses to think.

> LADY ASHTON
> James, you might not but act apace.
> You are in danger. Go now to
> Whitehall. Talk to Cromwell's
> daughter, Lady Claypole. She is her
> father's favourite and oft
> intercedes with the Protector for
> political offenders. There are many
> prisoners she got freed even though
> the laws had condemned them.

> HARRINGTON
> I know not Lady Claypole. Yet I am
> told she acts the part of a
> princess very naturally and obliges
> all persons with her civility. My
> thanks, Elizabeth. I shall attempt
> to convince her *Oceana* is no threat
> to her father.

INT. WHITEHALL PALACE - THAT AFTERNOON

Harrington sits in the antechamber of Cromwell's daughter,
LADY CLAYPOLE, who is twenty-seven years old. There are
several LADIES-IN-WAITING, with one attending to a small
child, MARTHA, who is four years old.

> HARRINGTON
> By your leave, do you know if Lady
> Claypole shall be much longer? I
> sent in my request for an audience
> some time since.

> A LADY-IN-WAITING
> It should'st not be, Mr.
> Harrington. My Lady was with her
> chaplain in prayer earlier. Belike
> she hath gone in to talk to her
> father. She often does so
> unannounced.
>   (MORE)

> A LADY-IN-WAITING (CONT'D)
> His Highness is so fond of her he
> drops his business presently so he
> can converse with her. He does this
> not with his other daughters.

> HARRINGTON
> And who is this child?

> A LADY IN WAITING
> She is Lady Claypole's youngest,
> Martha. I attend her closely as she
> is prone to illness. My Lady fears
> she may see an early death.

Harrington rises and walks over to Martha.

> HARRINGTON
> Good day, Martha. I am Mr.
> Harrington and I am hither to see
> thy mother. Are those thy dolls,
> Sweetheart? They are so handsome.
> Martha, would you like to hear a
> riddle some other children told me
> of late? What needs to be broken
> before you can use it?

> MARTHA
> I am afeared I know not, Sir.

> HARRINGTON
> An egg.

Martha smiles.

> MARTHA
> Doest thou know any better riddles,
> Mr. Harrington?

> HARRINGTON
> I know but one more. What makes an
> octopus laugh? Ten tickles. You
> see, ten tickles - tentacles, which
> an octopus has but I'm told by an
> excellent authority they are very
> limbs.

Martha laughs.

> MARTHA
> I knew that, Mr. Harrington. An
> octopus hath limbs not tentacles.

69.

                    HARRINGTON
          Yet do you know how an octopus
          moves? Let me show.

Harrington picks up Martha and begins tossing her gently so
her arms fling one way and back, and then up and down. Martha
and Harrington are laughing. Lady Claypole enters.

                    LADY CLAYPOLE
          James Harrington, I presume?

Harrington sets Martha down and steps forward.

                    HARRINGTON
          Madam, 'tis well you are come at
          this nick of time, or I had stolen
          this little lady.

                    LADY CLAYPOLE
          Stolen her? Pray, what would you do
          with her? For she is yet too young
          to become your mistress.

                    HARRINGTON
          Madam, though her charms assure her
          of a more considerable conquest,
          yet I must confess it is not love
          but revenge that prompts me to
          commit this theft.

                    LADY CLAYPOLE
          What injury have I done to you that
          you would steal my child?

                    HARRINGTON
          None at all. But you might be
          induced to prevail upon your father
          to do me justice, by restoring my
          child he has stolen.

                    LADY CLAYPOLE
          But that is impossible. My father
          would never do such a thing as he
          has enough children of his own. He
          would never take yours.

                    HARRINGTON
          I do not speak of the issue of my
          body but rather of my brain which
          Mr. Thurloe has misrepresented to
          the Lord Protector and taken out of
          the press by his order.

                    LADY CLAYPOLE
Is this the book *The Commonweath of
Oceana* of which I heard? I was told
by Thurloe himself it was damning
of my father.

                    HARRINGTON
I assure you it is only a political
romance, so far from any treason.
In fact, if it be restored to me, I
am willing to dedicate it to Oliver
himself and promise that you and he
shall be given the first copies.

                    LADY CLAYPOLE
Thurloe has told my father so many
lies. His hands are far too
drenched in innocent blood. But I
believe, Mr. Harrington, you are
one who tells what is true. What is
Oceana really about?

                    HARRINGTON
In a word, *Oceana*'s purpose is to
heal and repair our broken and war-
weary country. It simply requests
your father prepare the way for an
ideal Commonwealth.

                    LADY CLAYPOLE
And what kind of place would be
this *Oceana*?

                    HARRINGTON
Oceana is as the Rose of Sharon,
and the Lilly of the Valley. She is
comely as the tents of Kedar, and
terrible as an army with banners.
Its constitution will last forever
and tyranny end. Wealth shall be
shared and every citizen will in
time have his villa. It shall be a
true republic with the rule of the
community, not a single person. An
empire of laws, not men. Its
government will be democratic and
will include the greatest freedom,
including liberty of conscience,
where every man is his own prince.

                    LADY CLAYPOLE
I am fairly well read, Mr.
Harrington.
                    (MORE)

>   LADY CLAYPOLE (CONT'D)
>   You may be the first person in this
>   modern age who doth not speak of
>   democracy in a pejorative way.
>   *Oceana* seems a place I should like
>   my Martha to grow up in, should she
>   live that long. I shall speak to
>   His Highness immediately.

Harrington sits down and waits. In a few minutes, Lady Claypole returns.

>   LADY CLAYPOLE (CONT'D)
>   Mr. Harrington, my father thanks
>   you for coming. Yet he wants you to
>   know he doth not much affect
>   constitution builders. He grew
>   tired of the late Parliament with
>   its constitution pedantries and
>   parchments. He says of you - in his
>   words - "this gentleman had like to
>   trepan me out of power but what I
>   have got by the sword I will not
>   quit for a little paper shot." I
>   told him I was well pleased with
>   your manner of address and honesty,
>   and you mean him no treason. My
>   father thinks you a heathen for
>   wanting to rid God from all
>   politics. Yet perhaps to humour me
>   and, with hopes you may be able to
>   bring a lasting peace to our
>   troubled country, he promised
>   *Oceana* will be restored to you. I
>   believe I have kept you from
>   prison, Mr. Harrington. But be
>   wary. There are many who receive a
>   political theory of freedom,
>   liberty of conscience and
>   opposition to tyranny shall aye be
>   a threat to the raison d'etat.
>   Martha and I bid you good day, Sir.

>   HARRINGTON
>   Thank you, Lady Claypole, for your
>   kindness and most noble
>   disposition.

INT. THE HOUSE OF COMMONS - THREE YEARS LATER, AFTERNOON

Harrington and Lady Ashton are standing, waiting to enter the chamber to watch the proceedings.

                         LADY ASHTON
It has been years since I visited
the House of Commons, James. I
loved watching Ralph perform his
parliamentary duties here and those
wild debates 'twixt the
Presbyterians and Cromwell, back
when Oliver was a Parliamentary man
as crossed to the tyrant he became.

                         HARRINGTON
Those times are gone, sister, as is
Oliver, who has been dead now these
past eight months. His son Richard
is also gone. We shall hark no more
of the Cromwells. The Commonwealth
has returned and the opportunity to
right our world is upon us. I
should not be more excited.

                         LADY ASHTON
You cannot be happy with this
restored Commonwealth, James.
Surely not.

                         HARRINGTON
The recalled Rump is yet a narrow
oligarchy. It trusts not the people
and puts private interests above
the public good. If it is ruined
through the want of democratic
orders, the world will say to all
posterity it was not the Rump that
needed to trust the people, but
that the people trusted the Rump.

Praisegod Barebones, also standing in the lobby, approaches.

                         BAREBONES
Good day, Harrington. The news is
Neville will be proposing a motion
to take evidence on a new
constitution. I hope those of us
who believe in the return of Jesus
shall not be excluded. It will not
be the first time we hath been shut
out. We saw that with Cromwell.
Such betrayal! I should have been
more wary. For all his talk of
making a godly kingdom, he laughed
at us behind closed doors.

                    HARRINGTON
          Mr. Barebones, I should like you to
          meet my sister, Lady Ashton.

                    BAREBONES
          An honour to meet you, My Lady.

                    HARRINGTON
          I insisted to Henry that you and
          the Fifth Monarchists be members of
          the committee. He agrees and shall
          not proceed with his motion if you
          are not included. The godly must
          feel safe in this new republic. Our
          greatest weakness is that we stand
          divided. It is time friends of the
          Commonwealth join together. All
          shades of opinion shall be
          represented.

                    BAREBONES
          Comforting to hear. But still
          difficult for us to work with any
          Harringtonians. Men don't need
          better laws. They need better
          hearts! I have urged you before to
          burn *Oceana* since otherwise it will
          continue to sin when you are no
          more able to sin and forever
          prevent the shadow of mercy from
          approaching you. "For to fighteth
          against the saints, there can be
          nor peace or quarter from the King
          of Kings".

Barebones begins coughing violently.

                    BAREBONES (CONT'D)
          Yet you have known me on all this
          before, Harrington. You are right.
          Republicans must now stand
          together. They may yet put me in
          the Tower, but I shall do all in my
          power to prevent a Restoration. By
          all accounts, the late King's son
          is leading an evil life in Paris
          and this might not but be exposed.
          Anyone proposing a Stuart
          restoration should'st be deemed
          guilty of high treason. Allegiance
          canst only be to Parliament,
          however sinful it may be. Good day.

Barebones moves away. Denbigh is also waiting to enter. He adjusts his spectacles and approaches.

                    DENBIGH
          Tidings, Harringtons! Lady Ashton,
          as beautiful as ever! Both come no
          doubt to hear Neville present his
          petition? *Oceana* has gained much
          celebrity these last years. I read
          all's thou write, James, with great
          assiduity, especially your
          pamphlets. History shall call this
          "The Harringtonian Moment".

                    HARRINGTON
          Good to see you, Basil. Thank you.
          Yes, my writings seem to have
          struck a match, although I am not
          sure how the army is reacting to my
          dogma that government must be by
          agreement of the people.

                    DENBIGH
          True. They are not fortunate with
          you, James. Oliver was ne'r
          enthralled when intellectuals
          lectured him on what to try, and
          neither do these generals whom
          Cromwell put in place.

                    LADY ASHTON
          The army cannot be trusted. Basil,
          should'st James flee London, as
          others have done?

                    DENBIGH
          That shall only play into their
          game, Elizabeth. Besides, they will
          hunt James down. But who cares
          about those military tyrants? The
          important thing is to have his
          ideas circulated. James, you are my
          friend and hast been these many
          years, so haply it is not
          impertinent for me to suggest you
          condense your thoughts into short
          aphorisms and provide advice on how
          to prevent another civil war. It
          shall make for better reading and
          may have more influence. I can show
          it to various people. Who knows how
          you may be rewarded? Look, the
          prayers of the House are finished.
                    (MORE)

                    DENBIGH (CONT'D)
          Allow us see how this Rump reacts
          to Neville's petition. Do you have
          your money for the Doorkeeper? Such
          hypocrisy even for a republic! The
          House excludes citizens from every
          part of the legislature but admits
          them here on the floor if they can
          pay the fee!

The DOORKEEPER is about to open the doors to the chamber of
the House of Commons.

                    DOORKEEPER
          Ladies and gentlemen, the Commons
          have now completed their prayers.
          Thou may enter to stand below the
          bar. Arrant quiet. As usual, ladies
          to the right, gentlemen to the
          left. Thank you. Thank you.

INT. HOUSE OF COMMONS CHAMBER - MOMENTS LATER

Having paid the Doorkeeper his fee, about twenty people enter
and proceed below the bar. The House, constructed like a
theater with four rows of seats one above each other, has
more than a hundred Members in attendance. They sit to the
left, right, and behind the Speaker's Chair. Most wear large
brimmed hats and cloaks. Presiding over the proceedings is
THE SPEAKER OF THE HOUSE OF COMMONS who sits on a raised
chair. He has no wig but wears a hat similar to other
Members. Two Clerks sit immediately in front of him. The Mace
is placed horizontally on the Clerk's Table.

                    SPEAKER OF THE HOUSE OF COMMONS
          The House recognizes the Member for
          Redding, the Honourable Henry
          Neville.

                    SOME HONOURABLE MEMBERS
          Are you here to ridicule us,
          Neville? To insult this chamber? To
          blaspheme religion?

                    SPEAKER OF THE HOUSE OF COMMONS
          Order! Order!

                    NEVILLE
          Mr. Speaker. No man can better
          defend Parliament's cause and the
          Protestant religion than I. You
          are the true father - I am only the
          child brought to your door.
                    (MORE)

                    NEVILLE (CONT'D)
          If some I have insulted in my
          pamphlets - like those Cavalier
          Members who are now so poor (I only
          said if you are to share a
          mistress, you must equally pay the
          score (laughter); or perhaps our
          newest colleague, the handsome,
          young Mr. Lenthall who hath the art
          to love if the women love him. I
          simply said he makes love one hour
          to you, then beats the brains of it
          out in a quarter (more laughter) -
          I meant but to humour. My one
          request is that Members put aside
          their self interest and act instead
          like statesmen. Allow this House
          once again secure the trust of the
          people.

Cries of Hear! Hear!

                    NEVILLE (CONT'D)
          Mr. Speaker and colleagues. I have
          the honour today to present a
          petition of divers, well affected
          persons regarding the form of
          government England should now take.
          Although this petition has but a
          few signatures, it would have been
          possible to secure many thousand
          more if this had been desirable.
          Your petitioners offer their
          principles to establish a prudent
          constitution. These are: First, the
          exercise of all just authority over
          a people ought, under God, arise
          from their own consent, shown by
          the use of a secret ballot.

Cries of Hear! Hear!

                    NEVILLE (CONT'D)
          Second, without a written
          constitution of stated orders, a
          government of men, instead of laws,
          cannot be trusted;

More cries of Hear! Hear!

                    NEVILLE (CONT'D)
          Third, popular government must be
          rightly balanced since a Parliament
          of a single legislative house will
          become an oligarchy.
                    (MORE)

                    NEVILLE (CONT'D)
Parliament should consist of two
houses, one a Senate and the other
an assembly. Fourth, their
membership must rotate with one
third chosen for one year; one
third for two years; and another
third for three years. And the
members so elected shall receive a
salary. Finally, religious
differences will be tolerated and
receive equal protection. Thank
you, Mr. Speaker.

Neville has his petition delivered to the Clerk's Table with
cheers of "Hear, Hear!" and the thumping of desks. An older
Member, SAMUEL GOTT, rises to catch the Speaker's eye.

            SPEAKER OF THE HOUSE OF COMMONS
The House recognizes Samuel Gott.

                    SAMUEL GOTT, M.P.
Through you, Mr. Speaker, may I ask
a question, Mr. Neville? Why not
admit your indebtedness to your
friend James Harrington for this
petition? These principles come
straight from his book *Oceana*. Or
did you have a finger in that pie,
as Mr. Hobbes hath said? Do you
really think this country is ready
for an immortal Commonwealth? For
me, I shall not go back to times
past, nor look forward to *Oceana*'s
Platonic Commonwealth, things that
are not, and never shall be. We go
about to grasp more; and lose that
which we would have.

                    NEVILLE
I thank the Member for his
question. My reply carries two
answers. First, I hide not my
indebtedness to my friend. Poets
are the unacknowledged legislators
of the world. No, Mr. Gott. Hobbes
is wrong. *Oceana* is Mr.
Harrington's culinary masterpiece.
Whatever lies ahead, he shall
remain the most distinguished of
our Commonwealthmen. And second,
while Harrington feels it an honour
to wrap himself in Plato's toga, he
has shown he goes his own way.
                    (MORE)

> NEVILLE (CONT'D)
> *Oceana* proves proper constitutions
> can achieve what Platonic education
> could never: stability with wisdom.

Some thumping of desks.

> NEVILLE (CONT'D)
> Gentlemen, there can be no doubt
> Harrington's views are gaining
> favour. A year ago, the Council of
> State appointed a committee to read
> *Oceana* and report on it. Many
> members of Oliver's Council say
> they are now converted to its
> teachings. Even humanity's greatest
> poet, John Milton, supports
> Harrington's principles. The
> Levellers have written they too are
> in favour. The Don of Oxford has
> declared: "I admire Harrington's
> model and am ready to cry out as it
> were the pattern of the Mount." The
> leaders of this House - Edmund
> Ludlow, Arthur Haselrig, Henry Vane
> - accept his ideas. Given the
> balance of wealth and property that
> now exists, the time has come for
> England to build an immortal
> Commonwealth. The generations of
> the future, and marry, of the
> world, shall forever thank us for
> our efforts.

> SPEAKER OF THE HOUSE OF COMMONS
> In receiving this petition, may I
> tell you, Mr. Neville, your
> colleagues find it without any
> private end and only for the public
> interest. It lies much upon this
> House to make such a settlement as
> may be most for the good of
> posterity; and that we are about
> that work and intend to go forward
> with it with as much expedition as
> may be. And as for your part, I am
> commanded to give you the thanks of
> this House accordingly. Next order,
> Mr. Clerk!

Harrington and Lady Ashton begin exiting the chamber.
Harrington signals goodbye to Neville who waves back.

                    LADY ASHTON
          So that is it? No more than a
          polite thanks? James, are you not
          disconcerted?

                    HARRINGTON
          Not in the least! I knew most
          Members liked not the idea of
          rotation. That would ruin them!
          Yet I have more determination than
          ever. I shall heed Denbigh's
          advice and digest *Oceana*'s main
          points into a new manuscript. With
          Denbigh circulating it, it shall be
          more widely read. And if the army
          tries another coup against
          Parliament and makes this room
          stand empty, I shall create a club
          in one of the coffee houses hither
          at Westminster to debate the
          problems of government. We shall be
          inclusive. All of the city's
          leading intellectuals will be
          invited, be they Cavaliers,
          Roundheads, or Fifth Monarchists.
          We shall meet every night and stage
          the greatest debates of the
          century!

EXT. ON THE STREET OUTSIDE THE HOUSES OF PARLIAMENT - MOMENTS
LATER

After bidding Denbigh goodbye, Lady Ashton and Harrington
exit Parliament.

                    LADY ASHTON
          Keep care, James. Despite these
          times which grip you so intensely,
          there are other matters you might
          also attend to, more important than
          thy politics. Make not twice the
          same mistake. Anne Darrell has
          returned from Paris. She is here
          in London and unattached. She has
          confided to me she longs to see you
          and urges safety. Haply it is not
          too late for you both to be
          married.

                    HARRINGTON
          Am I to be wounded once again by
          Anne Darrell?
                         (MORE)

HARRINGTON (CONT'D)
At Holdenby, I told the late King I
had unwisely left her behind to go
on my Tour. Yet now I am too caught
in the spirit of the revolution to
hie back in time. No, Elizabeth. I
shall not see Anne Darrell. My
personal life counts nothing. The
library and coffee house club are
all that owe me. We might not but
build now our equal Commonwealth.
The old order of unwritten
constitutions, unelected second
houses, and self-interested
political factions must be swept
away. For the first time, the
people shall be placed above the
King or Parliament. Would we fail
to act, England shall be stuck with
them for the next four hundred
years.

LADY ASHTON
A sister's love for her brother
doth not forebear. Yet I think you
make a mistake not to embrace me as
a matchmaker. Politics may be
important yet not as vital as
matters of the heart. Allow us pray
history does not record another sad
story of these times - the tragic
life of James Harrington.

INT. HOLLAND, EXILE COURT OF KING CHARLES II - THREE DAYS
LATER

Edward Hyde, Lord Chancellor in exile, is with his Secretary.

SECRETARY TO THE LORD CHANCELLOR
Another cypher from London, Lord
Chancellor. 'Tis dated July 7 yet
no signature.

HYDE
I know who it is from. No doubt
tidings about the petition Henry
Neville presented on behalf of
Harrington and his friends a few
days since.

SECRETARY TO THE LORD CHANCELLOR
Who is sending you these, Mr. Hyde?

                         HYDE
My "spy", who else? 'Tis not
difficult to get information when
you make promises. I reach out
everywhere for what the Prince may
use for his benefit and mine. After
the King's son takes back the
throne, by God, there shall be a
reckoning. May you read it?

            SECRETARY TO THE LORD CHANCELLOR
Aye, Sir. "Neville and Harrington
hath set on foot a petition that
will breed bad blood. It will stir
the army to dissolve Parliament
with some outrage. Yesterday it was
presented to the Parliament a
Commonwealth model framed by
various well-wishers of the
republic. A doggerel is now
capturing London sounding like
this: 'Scot, Neville and Vane/With
the rest of the train/Are into
Oceana fled/Sir Arthur the
brave/That's as arrant a knave/Has
Harrington in his head'."

                         HYDE
That last part is referring to
Arthur Haselrig. He was one of
those five Members the late King so
foolishly tried to arrest when he
barged into the Commons and ordered
the Speaker to identify them.
Haselrig dominates the Rump with
his verbosity yet when he rises to
speak to a matter, he never speaks
to the matter! So even he is for
Harrington. I hope he is content to
lose his estates when we are
restored and he be put in the
Tower.

            SECRETARY TO THE LORD CHANCELLOR
And Harrington? What shall you do
about him?

                         HYDE
Charles Stuart has been made well
aknown by his friends that many are
now taken with Harrington's model.
I will bide my time. Public opinion
hath shifted. The Royalists will be
back in London within a year.
                    (MORE)

                    HYDE (CONT'D)
          I shall see to it republicanism is
          brought to its knees with
          imprisonments and executions. There
          will be no more *Oceanas*.

INT. BBC TELEVISION STUDIO, LONDON - SAME EVENING

Orwell, cigarette in hand, goes on with Harrington's story.

                    INTERVIEWER
          So how long did the restored
          Commonwealth last, Mr. Orwell?

                    ORWELL
          Only a few more months after
          Neville presented his petition.
          Although they did agree to prepare
          a new constitution, the Members
          argued bitterly among themselves.
          They were scattered into two camps
          - either Harrington or scripture.
          They then quarrelled with the army.
          By October, it was over. The army
          marched into London and locked
          Parliament's doors. But Harrington
          remained undeterred. As he told his
          sister, he created a club at Miles'
          Coffee House, and its meetings were
          packed. People said their debates
          were the smartest ever heard, that
          the arguments of the old Parliament
          were flat compared to theirs.
          Probably the best debate was the
          one between Harrington himself and
          Matthew Wren, his leading
          contemporary opponent. It's a
          little windy but worth noting since
          it pretty much summarized what
          England's disagreements boiled down
          to. Even Samuel Pepys, the famous
          diarist, was there that night, and
          he had brought an important guest.

EXT. LONDON, RESIDENCE OF SAMUEL PEPYS - EVENING

WILLIAM PENN, age fifteen, arrives at the door of his
neighbour, SAMUEL PEPYS. Pepys has promised to take his young
friend to Harrington's Rota Club.

                    PENN
          Mr. Pepys? Mr. Samuel Pepys? Are
          you ready Sir?

                    PEPYS
          Indeed I am, young Mr. Penn. My
          periwig is properly on, my coat is
          warm, and I have my purse with me.
          How is your darling mother and
          sister Peg? Such handsome females,
          both of them.

Pepys and Penn begin walking.

                    PENN
          Well enough I suppose, Sir. My
          father sends his greetings but has
          now left on some sort of foreign
          mission. Where, he would not say.

                    PEPYS
          No. The Admiral keeps his secrets
          close. I suspect it has something
          to do with the late King's son
          sitting over there in Holland with
          Hyde, itching to be restored to
          what he thinks is his inheritance -
          the English Throne. We shall see
          how this plays out. Yet tonight,
          Billy, we are off to Miles' Coffee
          House. I promised you an experience
          not easily forgotten. You are about
          to witness a meeting of the famous
          Rota Club of which I am proud to
          say I am a paying member. I hear
          you shall be attending Oxford and
          that your father wants you to study
          law. Look upon tonight as a
          preparation for thy studies.

                    PENN
          What exactly is the Rota Club, Mr.
          Pepys?

                    PEPYS
          It is a philosophical club where
          gentlemen come at night to divert
          themselves with political
          discourse, and to see the way of
          balloting. It is the contrivance of
          England's foremost republican,
          James Harrington. Now that the Rump
          has once more been put out,
          Harrington feels it important to
          have public meetings where the most
          intelligent Londoners debate what
          model of government is right for
          England.

                         PENN
          Who attends, Sir?

                         PEPYS
          Prominent Commonwealthmen,
          Royalists, military officers,
          economists, clergymen, peers from
          the House of Lords, eminent
          scientists, and those who just wish
          to observe, such as I. Miles hath
          built a round oval table with a
          passage in the middle so he can
          deliver his coffee. Hopefully you
          will get to hear Harrington speak.
          I fear his Club shall not be in
          existence much longer. Your father
          would know better, but I am hearing
          General Monck and his five thousand
          troops are about to stage another
          coup. They aim to take us from this
          anarchy. This may be the last time
          Harrington ever addresses the
          English people about his *Oceana*.

INT. MILES' COFFEE HOUSE, WESTMINSTER - SAME EVENING

Pepys and Penn enter the Club. The room is full. Harrington
is seated at the debating table next to Neville. A heated
discussion is taking place. Someone is speaking while the
audience makes comments like "No, never", and "Hear, hear!"
Miles continuously serves coffee. Harrington leaves to get a
glass of water.

                         PEPYS
          Come, Billy. This way. Harrington
          has just risen from the table. Let
          us make a quick introduction.
          Hello, James. James!

Harrington pours himself a glass of water.

                         HARRINGTON
          Oh, tidings Samuel. Glad to see
          you. We will be put out soon, I
          fear. Might be worth a jot in your
          diary. I spoke with Lord Dorset who
          suggested if Monck moves tonight,
          we should'st regard getting another
          place like the Cockpit, yet I
          believe that would come to nothing.
          And who is this young gentleman,
          Mr. Pepys?

                         PEPYS
          James Harrington, I should like you
          to meet my neighbour, young William
          Penn, the son of Admiral Penn, who
          will undoubtedly be our next
          Commissioner of the Navy.

                         PENN
          An honour to meet you, Mr.
          Harrington. Mr. Pepys has been
          telling me how the Rota Club
          conducts its business.

                         HARRINGTON
          And an honour to meet you, Mr.
          Penn. The future of our
          Commonwealth lies in the hands of
          our youth. I am glad you are here.
          If this age fails me, let us hope
          the next will do me justice. Yes,
          the Rota has a vigorous agenda. It
          is our custom to dispute
          everything, how plain or obscure,
          by knocking argument against
          argument, and then referring it to
          our wooden oracle, the ballot box,
          where democratic things are
          resolved. My fullest pardon, young
          William and Samuel, but I must
          return to my place. They may want
          me to close tonight's debate. But
          join us afterward. Neville and I
          usually attend the Rhenish Wine
          House.

Harrington returns to the table while Pepys and Penn take
their seats. The next debater is MATTHEW WREN, thirty years
old. The CHAIRMAN of the Rota Club, introduces him.

                         CHAIRMAN
          We shall now hear from Matthew
          Wren, the well-known scholar from
          Cambridge and Oxford. He told me
          earlier if Hyde ere returns, he
          intends to make Matthew his
          principal secretary. I am unsure
          whether condolences or
          congratulations are in order. Be
          wary, Matthew, Hyde's power not
          corrupt you!

Boos and cheers are heard. Wren stands to take the floor.

                    WREN
          Thank you, Mr. Chairman. I see you
          are one who "Hydes" nothing. But I
          rise tonight to speak not about me
          or my future but about the most
          important thing this English
          "revolution" has produced, a book
          called *Oceana*.

Wren holds up a copy of *Oceana*.

                    WREN (CONT'D)
          It portrays a Commonwealth that is
          immortal. Let me tell you,
          gentlemen, *Oceana* will heal not.
          James claims to have made two
          discoveries - that of the balance
          of dominion; and that of dividing
          and choosing. Yet his theory is
          based on faulty evidence. All Mr.
          Harrington has done is given the
          world a cause to complain about
          their own personal troubles. His
          plan to ensure there is a balance
          of wealth would so plume the
          nobility they would be just as
          strong of wing as wild fowl in
          moulting time. His agrarian economy
          is unnatural. It leaves a
          Commonwealth of cottagers at the
          beggar's bush. Instead of one
          sovereign, with power to stamp out
          sedition the moment it hath risen,
          there will be the rule of the
          ignorant many. Parliamentarians
          would be fetched from the dung cart
          to make laws, from the alehouse and
          the Maypole to dispose of our
          religion, our lives, and our
          estates. Why should we equalize
          unskillful rustics that never study
          politics a day? This leads but to
          anarchy.

Cries of "No, No! James doesn't say this!" Other cries of
"Hear! Hear!"

                    WREN (CONT'D)
          It is the great personages who
          should practice our politics, those
          sitting at the helm of affairs who
          comprehend the nature of
          government.
                    (MORE)

                    WREN (CONT'D)
          It is not for private men sitting
          in their cabinets, like Mr.
          Harrington, racking their brains
          about models of government.

Someone yells "That's not fair, Matthew."

                    WREN (CONT'D)
          As for dividing and choosing, James
          views politics as nothing more
          simple than two silly girls
          dividing a cake, trying to find a
          common interest. How big a piece
          may we both get and yet remain
          friends? He portrays Machiavel in
          puff paste, a Commonwealth come out
          of a bakehouse where smocks are the
          boulters. He fails to see politics
          as nothing more than the division
          of material spoils. ˜Tis rare there
          be a common interest. The
          concernments of the several parts
          of this nation are very different
          in reference to property and
          riches. Instead of trying to mine a
          common good, the purpose of
          politics limits itself to balancing
          competing interests. Thank you, Mr.
          Chairman.

Shouts of "Hear, Hear"; "Hyde will be pleased"; "No more
royalist noise;" "We died for democracy"; "Let's hear from
Harrington"; "Take the floor, James!"

                    CHAIRMAN
          Methinks our Club believes it
          should now hear from Mr. Harrington
          who shall close our debate.

Harrington stands.

                    HARRINGTON
          Thank you, Chairman, and thank you,
          Matthew. I am aware you are one of
          the virtuosi which meets at Gresham
          College to discuss learned and
          scientific matters. They have an
          excellent faculty for magnifying a
          louse and diminishing a
          Commonwealth.

Laughter.

                    HARRINGTON (CONT'D)
              But you are right Mr. Wren. I pray
              England can build a true
              Commonwealth. While most republics
              decay, *Oceana* shall be immortal. My
              concern has always been to bring
              peace to this nation. Yet a peace
              that shall endure. As did the
              Florentine, I hoped to develop a
              constitution that would see human
              beings as they are, not as they
              should be. As far as the agrarian
              goes, the equality of estates
              causeth the equality of power, and
              the equality of power is the
              liberty not only of the
              Commonwealth but of every man. We
              must establish a democracy, where
              all power is in the people and
              liberty of conscience is its own
              state.

Camera focuses on Penn looking as if he sees truth revealed
for the first time.

                    HARRINGTON (CONT'D)
              Liberty is indivisible. A free
              mind, a free speech, the freedom to
              worship God as thou pleases, and a
              free State must go together.
              Without liberty of conscience,
              civil liberty cannot be perfect.
              And without civil liberty, liberty
              of conscience cannot be perfect.
              To impose religious uniformity will
              only create tumult and destroy the
              social order. England has suffered
              this too long. Religion not
              according to a man's conscience can
              as to him be none at all.

Camera goes back on Harrington.

                    HARRINGTON (CONT'D)
              As for my political fable of two
              silly girls, I know it is set apart
              from the pomposities of university
              scholars. Matthew thinks I am being
              too simple. But am I, Mr. Wren?
              When politics is baked, does it not
              boil down to who gets the land, the
              commerce, the money? A Commonwealth
              is hardly a simple structure.
                        (MORE)

                    HARRINGTON (CONT'D)
In its core, it differs not from
Leviathan which also says to
imitate the human body. I have
tried to replicate famous Harvey so
that Parliament be a heart,
consisting of two ventricles. Each
performs a different craft. An
elected Senate which divides, and
an elected Assembly which chooses.
This shall be the organ to find our
common interest.

Cries of "Hear! Hear!"

                    HARRINGTON (CONT'D)
As to Mr. Wren's belief that a
political grandee is superior to a
citizen, such is intolerable. To
say a man may not write of
government except he be a
magistrate, is as absurd as to say,
a man may not make a sea chart
unless he is a pilot. It is known
Christopher Columbus made a chart
in his cabinet and found the Indys.
The magistrate that was good at his
steerage never took ill of him that
brought him a chart.

Harrington stops to drink some water.

                    HARRINGTON (CONT'D)
As for his declaration that
democracy shall lead to anarchy,
this need not be so. We cannot
measure a Commonwealth by the
boundless passions of men but only
by its laws, without which a free
people can no otherwise have a
course than a free river without a
proper channel. I have told a story
of my travels to some gentlemen and
they were pleased with it. Among
these at Rome I saw at their
carnival a pageant that represented
a kitchen. The cooks were cats and
kitlings, set in such frames, so
tried and ordered the poor
creatures could make no motion to
get loose, but the same caused them
to turn the spit, another to baste
the meat, a third to scim the pot,
and a fourth to make green sauce.
                    (MORE)

> HARRINGTON (CONT'D)
> If the frame of your Commonwealth
> be not such, as causeth every one
> to perform his certain function as
> necessarily as this did the cat to
> make green sauce, it is not right.
> Give us good orders, and they will
> make us good men.

The Rota Club is silent.

> HARRINGTON (CONT'D)
> Beware, my friends. General Monck
> is at the gate and our Commonwealth
> is hearing its death-knell.
> Undoubtedly, this shall be our last
> meeting. The late King's son, with
> the "little king" Hyde directing
> him, will soon be in power. Forget
> not! Those who dare trust men, do
> not understand men; and they that
> dare not trust laws or orders do
> not understand a Commonwealth!

Harrington sits down. Loud thumping, clapping and cheering.
Many come to shake Harrington's hand. Neville embraces him.
William Penn shows his utter admiration.

INT. HOUSES OF PARLIAMENT - TWO YEARS LATER, MAY

The Commonwealth has been dissolved and the Stuart monarchy
restored. The new King, Charles II, proceeds to open his
first Parliament.

The proceedings take place in the House of Lords. Its chamber
is a long, narrow room with tapestries on the walls. Matting
covers the floor. There is a small round window above the
throne. The Lords are dressed in their scarlet wool robes
and sit on benches. Seated in the middle are the justices of
the Courts, also in their robes. The Members of the House of
Commons are standing at the end of the chamber below the bar.
KING CHARLES II, thirty-one years old, is dressed in white, a
jeweled crown on his head. He is accompanied by heralds who
carry his long, crimson cape. Accompanying the King is the
Lord Chancellor, Edward Hyde. When the King enters, all
stand. Drums and trumpets are heard. Charles takes his seat
on a raised throne. Hyde, wearing a black velvet robe and
carrying in a purse the Great Seal, stands to the right. All
sit.

                        CHARLES II
          My Lords, and Gentlemen of the
          House of Commons, I am grateful our
          monarchy has been rightfully
          restored and the anarchy of the
          Commonwealth ceased. I shall not
          spend time telling you why I called
          you hither. I shall leave that to
          my Chancellor, Edward Hyde, who was
          advisor to my late father, so
          indecently executed by traitors who
          yet must punished for their crime.
          I assure you I will go to the Tower
          personally to interrogate them once
          they are caught. And we shall catch
          them, even if they are hiding in
          the wilds of America. Gentlemen,
          rest assured I shall concur with
          you in all things that prevent any
          disturbance that threatens the
          public peace. In God's name,
          together we will provide full
          remedies for any future mischiefs
          and will be severe against any new
          offenders, especially if they be so
          upon old principles. We shall pull
          up those principles by the roots.
          May God bless you all.

Hyde kneels before the King, then rises, and speaks.

                        HYDE
          The King called you hither by his
          writ which is the only lawful way
          to the meeting of a Parliament. God
          must be thanked for providing a day
          like today that many good men had
          died praying for - seeing a King at
          the opening of the Parliament. Our
          nation is still racked by the
          illness of the plague and there are
          numerous physicians working
          tirelessly. Kings are like
          physicians who practice the same
          diligence. This King will use all
          indulgence to restore his patients
          to health. But there are sorts of
          patients who deserve none of his
          lenity. These are seditious book
          writers and pamphleteers,
          politicians and preachers who
          continually reproach against our
          laws.
                        (MORE)

                    HYDE (CONT'D)
          Rest assured our new King will
          provide new remedies for new
          diseases. His government will
          secure the precious person of the
          Sovereign from the first approaches
          of villainy; and the peace of the
          kingdom from the first overtures of
          sedition.

Hyde kneels, then rises. The King rises and all stand. The
drums and trumpets begin again. Charles and Hyde exit the
chamber. Hyde goes into a private room where his new
Secretary, Matthew Wren, is waiting.

                    WREN
          Your "spy", Lord Chancellor, has
          arrived. I put him in the adjoining
          room.

                    HYDE
          Well done, Matthew. Hopefully he
          has come unseen. I shall greet him
          now.

Hyde enters the adjoining room. The camera focuses on Hyde's
face, not that of the "spy". His identity remains unknown.

                    HYDE (CONT'D)
          We have met once before. Your work
          when I was in exile proved most
          useful. Wren has given you your
          money. And you must not worry. The
          security of your possessions shall
          be granted. Now it is time for you
          to become a provocateur. Remember
          to keep your identity hidden and
          let none suspect you are working
          with the King. I have endured too
          long the philosophical rantings of
          the intellects of the Commonwealth.
          Particularly the author of *Oceana*,
          whom you know. It is time these
          Commonwealthmen be removed. And
          that includes the religious
          fanatics. You know about whom I am
          talking. You must trap these
          traitors in one coup, especially
          Harrington. Very simply, we shall
          forge a conspiracy these
          retrogrades are plotting
          assassinations, including murdering
          our King. They will be accused of
          meeting regularly in taverns, like
          the Bow Street tavern.
                    (MORE)

                         HYDE (CONT'D)
          Bribe one of the servants there or
          do whatever thou must to get
          someone to testify they have seen
          them making speeches about
          promoting a change in government
          and restoring the Rump. Do your
          treachery well. The future of
          England depends on it. Harrington
          and his crowd must be silenced!

Hyde leaves the room.

EXT. BIRDCAGE WALK - SEVEN MONTHS LATER, MORNING

Lady Ashton runs from her carriage towards Harrington's
house. After failing to open the door, she bangs on it.

                         LADY ASHTON
          Hello! Hello! Is anyone there?
          Jessy, open up!

                         JESSY
          My Lady! I sent the boy to fetch
          thee. Something terrible has
          happened! Soldiers came early this
          morning and dragged Mr. Harrington
          away. He was in his library. They
          knocked not. Just burst in and
          pulled him onto the street, with
          his papers. I fear the worst. I
          sent right away for you and Mr.
          Neville.

                         LADY ASHTON
          Henry comes now. Who is he with?
          Denbigh?

                         NEVILLE
          Elizabeth.

Neville and Lady Ashton embrace.

                         NEVILLE (CONT'D)
          When the boy came, I went and got
          Basil. He has news.

Denbigh adjusts his spectacles.

                         DENBIGH
          Lady Ashton. I know you are
          distressed. We all are. I am
          acquainted with Hyde - I negotiated
          with him at Uxbridge.
                         (MORE)

DENBIGH (CONT'D)
And I know Matthew Wren. I met with
him earlier today. He tells me Hyde
has ordered the arrest of James
with seven other Commonwealthmen
who meet regularly at Nonsuch
Tavern. They shall be charged with
treasonable designs and practices.
The warrant includes Praisegod
Barebones. Hyde hath evidence they
are all involved in anti-royalist
plots. Apparently one of the
servant girls, a Mary Ellis, gave a
statement she heard Harrington make
a speech saying the present
government must be changed and the
Rump restored. The girl was
obviously frightened but stuck with
her story. Hyde says the
Commonwealthmen are planning a
further meeting next month and
bringing in arms.

NEVILLE
Such stupidity. James ne'r goes to
Nonsuch House. I do, but he does
not. And they have not arrested me.
I know they are opening my letters
yet there is nought to find.

DENBIGH
Give them time, Henry. They shall
find an excuse and bring thee as
well before the Examiners.

NEVILLE
Maybe they have the wrong
Harrington. There were others who
served the Commonwealth, as you
know.

DENBIGH
I asked Wren that. The warrant said
Sir James Harrington. Wren said
although they might be mistaken in
title, he doubted if they would be
mistaken of his guilt.

LADY ASHTON
The Nonsuch Tavern, Basil? T'is a
place frequented by Fifth
Monarchists. All its servants go on
Sundays to the Lock and Key. And
Barebones hath too been arrested?
Could this be a ploy?
(MORE)

                    LADY ASHTON (CONT'D)
James was much too friendly to
Barebones. Far too trustworthy. He
hates my brother and is a notorious
schismatic. I personally known him
say *Oceana* is a sinful book and
should'st be burned. Barebones is
ill. Could he have betrayed James
and then bargained for an early
release? Shall I go see this Mary
Ellis?

                    DENBIGH
I advise not. They shall say you
are interfering with a witness and
arrest you.

                    LADY ASHTON
May I then at least go to the Tower
to see James? He may want a doctor.

                    DENBIGH
No. None are allowed to come to his
sight or speech. 'Tis better we
wait. I hear Lord Lauderdale has
been appointed a Commissioner to
interview him. Maybe there are
things we do not know.

                    NEVILLE
They can put you in the Tower
forever. Allow us do what we can to
get James a speedy trial. At least,
grant him a chance to prove his
innocence.

                    LADY ASHTON
This is no better than the late
King's execution. James is seen as
a danger to this restored monarchy
as Charles was to the Commonwealth.
Hyde wants no more *Oceanas*. He
shall dispatch my brother to make
sure that happens.

INT. TOWER OF LONDON - DECEMBER, 1661, NIGHT

LORD LAUDERDALE, age forty-five, a Commissioner appointed to
investigate the plot, enters Harrington's prison cell.
Harrington rises. Lauderdale sits. Lauderdale speaks with a
Scottish accent.

                    LORD LAUDERDALE
Harrington.

                    HARRINGTON
Lord Lauderdale.

                    LORD LAUDERDALE
I have been appointed a
Commissioner to examine these
charges you endeavored in several
meetings to promote a change in
government. The King thinks it
strange that, ever since he came
over from Holland and let you live
so quiet, you be now so ungrateful.
Were you so much affronted you
should enter into such desperate
practices?

                    HARRINGTON
Lord Lauderdale, when I know why
you say this, I shall know what to
say.

                    LORD LAUDERDALE
Do you know Praisegod Barebones?

                    HARRINGTON
Yes, My Lord.

                    LORD LAUDERDALE
When did you see him?

                    HARRINGTON
I think I called at his shop thrice
in my life.

                    LORD LAUDERDALE
Have you ever had meetings with him
since the King came over?

                    HARRINGTON
No, My Lord.

                    LORD LAUDERDALE
That is so at angles to what I have
been told! Did you go into any
tavern with him?

                    HARRINGTON
No, My Lord.

                    LORD LAUDERDALE
This, Sir, is very hard to believe.
Come, Harrington. It will do you
no good.
                    (MORE)

                    LORD LAUDERDALE (CONT'D)
          Had you not, in March last, a
          meeting with Barebones at Nonsuch
          House? Were there not about twenty
          more of you? We have a witness who
          said you made a speech about half
          an hour long that you betake
          yourselves into one task which was
          to dissolve this Parliament, and
          bring in a new one, or the old one
          again? Was this meeting not
          adjourned from thence to Mill Bank
          and were you not there also?

                    HARRINGTON
          My Lord, I know not who told you
          but if you think these things are
          true, I have no refuge but to the
          mercy of God and of the King.

                    LORD LAUDERDALE
          This, Harrington, is true.

                    HARRINGTON
          Well then, My Lord, solemnly and
          deliberately, I renounce the mercy
          of God and the King, if any of this
          be true.

                    LORD LAUDERDALE
          Do you know Mr. Henry Neville?

                    HARRINGTON
          Very well, My Lord.

                    LORD LAUDERDALE
          When did you see him?

                    HARRINGTON
          My Lord, I seldom used to visit
          him. But when he was in town,
          usually when the Parliament met, he
          used to see me at my house every
          morning.

Lauderdale pauses. He then speaks, not looking at Harrington.

                    LORD LAUDERDALE
          Come, Harrington, you had better
          confess these things.

                    HARRINGTON
          My Lord, look upon me. Do you not
          know an innocent face from a guilty
          one? You do, My Lord.
                         (MORE)

                    HARRINGTON (CONT'D)
          Everyone does. My Lord, you are a
          great man. You come from the King
          but you are a messenger of death.
          If I be a malefactor, why am I not
          pale? Why do I not tremble? Why
          does not my tongue falter? Why have
          you not taken me tripping? My Lord,
          these are unavoidable symptoms of
          guilt. Do you find such things in
          me?

Lauderdale again pauses.

                    LORD LAUDERDALE
          No. I have said all I think I have
          to say.

                    HARRINGTON
          My Lord, but I have not.

                    LORD LAUDERDALE
          Come then. Speak.

                    HARRINGTON
          This is a practice, a practice for
          innocent blood. Ah, My Lord, if you
          have taken half the pains to
          examine the guilty that you have
          done to examine the innocent, you
          had found it. It could not have
          escaped you. My Lord, for your own
          sake, the King's sake, let such
          villains be found out and punished.

Lauderdale rises.

                    LORD LAUDERDALE
          Why if it be as you say, they
          deserve punishment enough, but
          otherwise it will come severely
          upon you. I will leave. It is late.

                    HARRINGTON
          Lord Lauderdale, now if I might, I
          would like to answer the preamble.

Lauderdale sits down.

                    LORD LAUDERDALE
          Come, say it.

                    HARRINGTON
My Lord, you charge me with being
in principles contrary to the
King's government. Others accuse me
of being a private man who meddled
with politics saying what has a
private man to do with politics?
But all that have written wisely on
government have been private men,
as my self. There is Aristotle,
there is Livy, there is Machiavel.
My Lord, I can sum up Aristotle's
book *The Politics* in a few words.
He says there is a barbarous
monarchy where people have no votes
in the making of laws, and there is
a heroic monarchy where people have
their votes in the making of laws.
He then says there is democracy and
affirms a man cannot be said to
have liberty but in a democracy
only.

Lauderdale shows impatience.

                 HARRINGTON (CONT'D)
I say, Aristotle says so. I have
not said as much. But under what
prince was it? Was it not
Alexander, the greatest prince then
in the world? I beseech you, My
Lord, did Alexander hang up
Aristotle? Did he molest him? One
of the fullest authors about
Commonwealths is Livy. Did he not
write under Augustus Caesar? Did
Caesar hang up Livy, did he molest
him? Was there not a greater
Commonwealthman than Machiavel? But
he wrote under the Medici when they
were princes in Florence. Did the
Medici hang up Machiavel? I have
done no different than as the
greatest politicians. The King
should do no otherwise than as the
greatest princes. Remember, I wrote
Oceana under a usurper, Oliver
Cromwell. I had been asked by a
most wise martyr who I will always
hold in great affection, to tell
Oliver and his followers what a
Commonwealth was because they did
not know. I never wrote against the
present King's government.
                     (MORE)

                    HARRINGTON (CONT'D)
          If the law could have punished me,
          Oliver would have done it. Therefor
          Oceana was not obnoxious to the
          law. After Oliver, the Parliament
          said they were a Commonwealth. I
          said they were not and proved it.
          The Parliament accounted me a
          Cavalier. Now the King makes me a
          Roundhead.

Lauderdale rises.

                    LORD LAUDERDALE
          These things you speak of are out
          of doors. If you be no plotter, the
          King does not reflect upon your
          writings.

                    HARRINGTON
          My Lord, it is my duty to wait on
          you no further.

Lauderdale exits.

EXT. TOWER OF LONDON - FIVE MONTHS LATER, MORNING

Lady Ashton arrives in a carriage, with her DRIVER. It is
raining heavily. There is a GUARD at the Tower's entrance.

                    LADY ASHTON
          Driver, please wait hither till my
          visit be done.

                    DRIVER
          Yes, My Lady.

Lady Ashton exits the carriage.

                    GUARD
          What is your business here?

                    LADY ASHTON
          I demand to see the Lieutenant of
          the Tower. My business deals with a
          prisoner, James Harrington, who was
          taken hither five months since. The
          sheriff is coming shortly with a
          Habeas Corpus duly granted by a
          judge. I am Harrington's sister. I
          want to speak to my brother.

                    GUARD
          It will doth little good yet I
          shall fetch the Lieutenant.

The LIEUTENANT OF THE TOWER arrives.

                    LIEUTENANT OF THE TOWER
          What doth thou desire in such fowl
          weather?

                    LADY ASHTON
          My name is Lady Ashton, wife of
          Ralph Ashton, the former Member of
          Parliament. I demand to see your
          prisoner, James Harrington. We have
          a *Habeas Corpus*. The sheriff
          arrives this afternoon with it. I
          have a gift of fifty pounds if you
          allow me see my brother now. We
          have tenants in Rand who refuse to
          pay their rent 'lest their landlord
          is proven still alive.

The Lieutenant takes her money.

                    LIEUTENANT OF THE TOWER
          I cannot let you see him, My Lady.
          Yet I shall allow you information.

                    LADY ASHTON
          Why not? The sheriff is coming to
          serve his warrant.

                    LIEUTENANT OF THE TOWER
          Because the prisoner is no longer
          here. The King's men had known you
          would be granted a motion so they
          moved your brother to another jail.
          'Tis a common practice. I have seen
          it done many times. This way they
          prevent his release and a trial.

                    LADY ASHTON
          But to which jail, Sir?

                    LIEUTENANT OF THE TOWER
          St. Nicholas Island, off Plymouth.

                    LADY ASHTON
          Plymouth. Yet that is four hundred
          miles away!

                    LIEUTENANT OF THE TOWER
          I was bid at two o'clock this
          morrow to get Harrington ready.
          They were going to put him secretly
          on a ship. I suspect it hath sailed
          already.

                    LADY ASHTON
          Please, Lieutenant, say to me how
          my brother is?

                    LIEUTENANT OF THE TOWER
          Not well, My Lady. Clearly his
          health has deteriorated. And his
          mind. There is a decline in
          discourse. He may have scurvy. At
          least that is what the prison
          doctor told me. He has been giving
          Harrington guaiacum in his coffee.
          In heavy doses. Too heavy in my
          opinion. It brings on madness.

                    LADY ASHTON
          My God! They are poisoning him.
          Hyde is bent on driving him insane
          so he can no longer write. What
          kind of prison does St. Nicholas
          Island have?

                    LIEUTENANT OF THE TOWER
          Far worse than hither, My Lady.
          Those jails have very narrow
          quarters and no fresh water. No
          matter what their crimes, I pity
          anyone imprisoned there.

Lady Ashton is shaken and on verge of tears.

                    LADY ASHTON
          I thank you, Sir.

She turns to leave.

                    LADY ASHTON (CONT'D)
          Say to me one more thing. Is the
          prisoner Praisegod Barebones still
          here?

                    LIEUTENANT OF THE TOWER
          Curious you should ask. Barebones
          was released two days since. They
          said 'twere on account of his poor
          health.

LADY ASHTON
My, Lieutenant. How strange a
coincidence is this!

She returns to her carriage.

DRIVER
Is thy visit finished, My Lady?

LADY ASHTON
Not quite. Prithee bring me to the
leather shop called the Lock and
Key. And grant me the coat pistol I
know you possess. I shall pay Mr.
Barebones a visit.

EXT. THE LOCK AND KEY - LATER THAT MORNING

Lady Ashton bangs on the shop's door. It is still raining.

LADY ASHTON
Barebones! Barebones! I demand to
talk to you!

Barebones is behind the closed door, coughing violently.

BAREBONES
The shop is not open. Read the
sign. Who is there?

LADY ASHTON
You had better open for me, you
fanatic. Should you refuse, you
shall be saying hello to Jesus. I
have a pistol and am afeared not to
use it. Allow me in. I am the
sister of James Harrington!

Barebones opens the door and coughs.

BAREBONES
I remember you. We met at the
Parliament when Neville presented
his petition. Harrington introduced
us. Lady Ashton, would I remember
correctly.

LADY ASHTON
For a sick man who gets released
early from prison when he is bore
for treason, you certainly have all
your faculties. I am coming in.

INT. INSIDE THE LOCK AND KEY - SECONDS LATER

Lady Ashton enters the shop.

                    BAREBONES
          Why so hostile, My Lady? The Lord
          frowns on souls with hatred in
          their hearts.

                    LADY ASHTON
          As I am sure He frowns on
          hypocrites who betray comrades
          fighting for like cause. My brother
          treated you with nought yet
          respect, despite your differences
          in philosophy. I knew James was in
          danger but ne'r thought it would be
          from a Commonwealthman!

                    BAREBONES
          With Christ as my witness, I was
          ne'r Harrington's enemy. He came
          into my shop at divers times yet
          our debate was always amicable. Our
          ways different, our goals not
          totally dissimilar.

                    LADY ASHTON
          Then why his betrayal?

                    BAREBONES
          What are thy grounds for saying
          such a thing?

                    LADY ASHTON
          Come, Pastor. Doth thou regard me
          stupid? His home was burst into
          fifteen months since by soldiers.
          He was dragged as a dog into the
          street and put in the Tower for
          conspiracy to overthrow the King's
          new government and was ne'r granted
          a trial.

                    BAREBONES
          Yet I faced liked circumstances
          just as un-Christian.

                    LADY ASHTON
          They said my brother had meetings
          with you and other Commonwealthmen
          at the tavern called Nonsuch House
          in Covent Garden.

                    BAREBONES
I told Hyde's men many times that
just because old Republicans are
accustomed to meet at such places
does not mean they are plotting to
disturb the nation's peace. I ne'r
had meetings with Harrington except
in my shop and then that day at the
House of Commons when you were
present.

                    LADY ASHTON
But there was also the evidence of
a young Mary Ellis who is an
admitted Fifth Monarchist and
attends your church regularly. She
told the authorities you, Neville,
and James, with others, often met
at Nonsuch. She said she heard my
brother give a speech about
Commonwealthmen working together to
dissolve the present Parliament and
bring back the Rump. Did you
convince Mary to say these things?
Were you working with Hyde and Wren
as an informer to save your own
skin, knowing that when the late
King's son returned, Hyde would
destroy the Fifth Monarchy men? Did
he make you a promise for early
release which just so happened two
days before Hyde secretly
transported my brother to that
ghastly jail off the coast of
Plymouth? Shall I go down to
Nonsuch House and re-interview Mary
Ellis with my barrister, or demand
the sheriff do it?

                    BAREBONES
That will do no good.

                    LADY ASHTON
Pray, tell why?

                    BAREBONES
Because Mary is dead. Three weeks
ago. There was a fight amongst a
group of soldiers. Too much
drinking. Pistols were discharged.
A ball struck Mary who was caught
in the skirmish. She died
instantly. One of her serving
friends told me it be no accident.
                    (MORE)

BAREBONES (CONT'D)
That a soldier aimed directly at
Mary's head. There will be no
investigation, of course. One death
more of a poor, young believer in
Christ's return means nothing. Her
demise has saddened me to the core.
She was a good girl but went
terribly astray. She was wrong. I
never attended any such meeting
with Harrington. He is too bookish
to get involved in plots. Someone
powerful must have frightened Mary
into providing that testimony. I
had hoped to talk to her but I was
confined in prison. Your ill
thoughts of me, Lady Ashton, are un-
deserving. I would never work with
Hyde or Wren. My beliefs have not
changed. The world has groaned
under the acts of tyranny committed
by Kings and their advisors.

LADY ASHTON
But why should I believe you?

BAREBONES
Because I am dying. It was my wife
who petitioned the new King I be
released, pleading my illness. I
think he is tiring of Hyde and his
rogue ways - forever attempting to
usurp his powers. Perhaps young
Charles took pity on me because
back in Oliver's time, I seemed
someone important. After the first
Rump fell, Cromwell called a
Parliament of Saints which they
called "The Barebones Parliament".
I was a leading member. It was to
be a godly legislature. We did some
good things, making marriages by
civil ceremony possible, and not
executing pick-pockets or horse
thieves for their first offence.
But the Parliament of Saints soon
collapsed, as did the three
Protectorates and the restored
Rump. Now the tyrant's son is back
on the throne. Sadly, in all this
turbulence, there has been a great
silence from heaven. I think I
shall stick for the time I have
left to my real profession which is
selling leather.

                    LADY ASHTON
          Then who betrayed my brother? Do
          you know?

                    BAREBONES
          It can only be a Royalist who
          disguises himself as a Republican.
          Who it is, we may never know. In
          this new world, spying, betrayal,
          and dirty hands shall henceforth
          be a common practice. All things
          Harrington fought against. If I am
          in despair, I pity thy brother.

EXT. ENTRANCE TO THE PRISON ON ST. NICHOLAS ISLAND - TWO
MONTHS LATER, MORNING

The EARL OF BATH, Governor of Plymouth, age thirty-four, is
greeted by the LIEUTENANT OF THE PRISON.

                    LIEUTENANT OF THE PRISON
          Good day, Governor. Beautiful day,
          Sir.

                    BATH
          Lieutenant, I am not hither for
          pleasantries. I have received
          correspondence from the wife of a
          former Parliamentarian, General
          Ralph Ashton, who says some rather
          unpleasant things about how one of
          our prisoners is being confined
          here. The prisoner is her brother,
          James Harrington. I am a reader,
          Lieutenant. Harrington is the
          author of *Oceana*. I used to attend
          his Rota Club when I visited
          London. I canst not receive such a
          brilliant and kind man as he is
          being mistreated in my prison.

                    LIEUTENANT OF THE PRISON
          'Tis not my doing, Governor. I was
          told by Whitehall Harrington be
          bore in close confinement and
          granted his medicines twice a day
          since he was at risk to escape and
          bring more treasonous actions upon
          our King.

                    BATH
          These were not my decrees,
          Lieutenant.
                    (MORE)

                    BATH (CONT'D)
          You report to me, not Hyde. Allow
          me see the prisoner immediately.

INT. HARRINGTON'S PRISON CELL - A FEW MINUTES LATER

The Lieutenant takes the Governor to Harrington's cell and
opens the door.

                    LIEUTENANT OF THE PRISON
          Beware, my Lord. The prisoner's
          mind is disordered.

                    BATH
          Harrington! Stand up, man. Look at
          me. I am the Governor of Plymouth,
          the Earl of Bath. I have heard from
          thy sister, Lady Ashton, that you
          are not well.

Harrington is lying against the wall in a small, cold, filthy
cell. He has lost considerable weight and has a fever. He is
perspiring. One side of his face has drooped and he has
difficulty speaking. When he hears the name of his sister, he
makes an attempt to get up but is unable to.

                    HARRINGTON
          Elizabeth? Be she with you, My
          Lord?

                    BATH
          No, Harrington. She has pleaded
          with me I bid the King to release
          you.

                    HARRINGTON
          Did you bring my medicine? I want
          not to be released. I summon only
          my medicine. The guards mix it in
          my coffee. Where is my coffee?

                    LIEUTENANT OF THE PRISON
          His medicine, Governor, is that
          mischievous drug, guaiacum. I was
          told to serve it to him twice a
          day. He already had some this
          morrow.

                    BATH
          I understand what is happening. All
          right, Lieutenant, I have seen
          enough.
                    (MORE)

                         BATH (CONT'D)
          Restrain his "medicine" presently
          and find the prison doctor. I am
          writing directly to Charles.

The Governor starts to leave.

                         HARRINGTON
          Wait! Leave not, Sir! Regard,
          Governor, see how I sweat. Look,
          look! My perspiration is turning to
          flies. Sometimes they turn to bees!
          Doth thou not see how they are
          coming from inside of me? They are
          evil spirits!

                         BATH
          No, James. They are not evil
          spirits. 'Tis only your
          imagination. I shall bid His
          Majesty to remove you from this
          place and back to London. Oh, I
          forget. Your sister asked I grant
          you this letter. She says it is not
          from her but from someone you used
          to know. Hither, I shall leave it
          towards the door.

The Governor and the Lieutenant leave the cell. Harrington
stays motionless on the floor, then slowly crawls to the
door. He opens the letter. It is simply a card with one
sentence: "I love you - Anne". Harrington smiles and then
weeps.

INT. WHITEHALL PALACE, HYDE'S OFFICE - TWO WEEKS LATER,
AFTERNOON

                         WREN
          Your "spy", Lord Chancellor, is
          waiting without. He wants to know
          if there is anything more to be
          done about this Harrington
          business.

                         HYDE
          I think, Matthew, this "Harrington
          business" has ran its course. I, or
          rather England, has got what we
          wanted. Apparently, the Governor of
          Plymouth heard about Harrington's
          condition and wrote the King his
          life would not be long if he were
          not removed to London.
                         (MORE)

                    HYDE (CONT'D)
Charles called me in last night to
say he is going to grant a warrant
for Harrington's release since, to
quote His Majesty, "nothing
appeared against him supported by
good proof or probable
presumptions." As if there ever
were! It appears this great
philosopher has become nothing more
than a cracked-brain, drug addicted
dipsomaniac. He is no longer a
threat to the State. Still, we
better keep him under surveillance.

                    WREN
Shall I let the "spy" know this?

                    HYDE
I shall tell him myself.

Hyde exits his office into a large hallway which has various
people walking in different directions. He speaks softly to
the "spy" who is unseen.

                    HYDE (CONT'D)
It is finished. Arrange to tell his
sister she can retrieve him in
Plymouth. There shall be no more
Oceanas. Harrington is in bedlam.
He is only a corpse waiting to be
sent back to the grave. Your work
is completed. The nation thanks
you. I shall make sure the King
rewards you with his letter patent
to elevate you to the peerage,
maybe make you a Viscount or a
Baron. That is not such bad
recompense, eh? And do not spend
time fretting over betrayals. You
and the rest of these Westminster
politicians had better start
learning morality will no longer be
the State's objective. Harrington
and Neville were fond of quoting
Machiavel. They both should have
heeded his warning that a prince,
if he wants to maintain himself,
must learn how not to be good.
Leave now. We shall speak no more.
Oh, by the way, you have dropped
your glasses. Here they are.

Audience sees the back of a tall, bulky man walking away.

EXT. HARRINGTON'S RESIDENCE, BIRDCAGE WALK, LONDON - THIRTEEN
YEARS LATER, SUMMER MORNING

William Penn knocks on Harrington's door. He is now thirty-
one years old and dressed in a black Quaker coat with collar
and cuffs, and a felt hat. Answering the door is ANNE
DARRELL, Harrington's wife. She is sixty-two, two years
younger than Harrington. She is fresh, healthy, and shapely,
with thick dark hair showing streaks of grey. The freckles on
her face are starting to fade.

                    ANNE
          Yes? May I help you, Sir?

                    PENN
          By your leave, Madam. I am looking
          for James Harrington, the author of
          Oceana. I would like to talk to
          him. My name is William Penn.

                    ANNE
          William Penn? The son of the late
          Admiral? You're the one who went to
          the Rota Club meeting with Mr.
          Pepys the night of General Monck's
          coming-in. Samuel keeps us privy
          about you. James told me he would
          like to meet you again. He is out
          in the garden with Henry Neville.
          Henry comes most mornings. Shall
          thou join us? My name is Anne.
          Anne Darrell. I am his wife.

Penn looks surprised, then takes off his hat.

                    PENN
          Most pleasant to meet you, Anne. I
          was unaware he had married.

                    ANNE
          Our marriage came terribly late,
          granted we have known each other
          since childhood, although for many
          years we saw not each other. We are
          such divers people. James loves his
          books. I care not for reading much.
          Yet still, when love is determined
          to enter the heart, it stays there
          forever, no matter what the
          circumstances.

                    PENN
          When did you marry?

                    ANNE
After his release from prison. You
are a Quaker, Mr. Penn. You know
something of prisons? And unjust
persecutions?

                    PENN
Alas, I do, Mrs. Harrington.
Particularly unheated prison cells.

                    ANNE
Yet at least they did not poison
you or make you an addict. It hath
taken James so long to rid himself
of his dependency on guaiacum. His
attacks were so severe. It pleases
me to tell you he has recovered.
Well, almost. The shock from the
late King's execution, it is my
belief, never went away, and his
rememberance now fades. He is
rational enough most days then
suffers delusions the spirits of
animals, like bees and flies, live
within his body and spring forth.
There is little the doctors can do.
Besides he would not heed them. He
hath an almost religious conviction
his hallucinations are real. He
even conducts experiments to
discover he is sane. Perhaps he is.
The mechanics of nature are still a
mystery, even in these modern
times. James always searched for
truth. If this be what he believes,
I shall ne'r dispute him. My love
for him is too great.

                    PENN
Mrs. Harrington, no matter what the
King's men have done, your
husband's writings shall live on.
My father used to say I am a man
who dreams dreams. My dreams are
built on *Oceana*'s foundations. I
canst not tell you enough how
influenced I was the night I heard
your husband speak at the Rota. I
want James to know I have an
opportunity to bring *Oceana* to
America which I hope will seed the
nation.

                         ANNE
          Then join this way. My guess is you
          smoke not. Sadly, I am corrupt to
          the bone so it is no sin for me. I
          shall fetch us all more coffee.

EXT. HARRINGTON'S GARDEN - A FEW MINUTES LATER

Anne leads Penn to the garden. Harrington has aged. Palsy is
setting in and he suffers from gout. Still he is alert and
cheerful. Neville has not changed, always fit and humorous.

                         ANNE
          James, Henry, we hast a visitor.
          The young boy who attended the Rota
          Club with Mr. Pepys that last
          night. He is now a man. William
          Penn.

Harrington stares at Penn.

                         HARRINGTON
          Penn? I remember an Admiral Penn,
          though he be definitely not a
          Quaker. I am sorry, Sir. I don't
          recall you.

                         NEVILLE
          Come, James. Young William Penn. He
          came with Samuel to the Rota that
          last night. We all then went for
          drink at the Rhenish House.

                         HARRINGTON
          The Rhenish? Yes, with Pepys. The
          young gentleman who was with him.
          Yes, yes. Of course. Uplifting to
          see you, Mr. Penn! Yet with sorrow
          I cannot lift myself to pay you
          homage. Please, sit and join us!

Penn sits. Anne pours coffee. She and Neville take snuff by
inhaling it in their noses, then with Harrington, light their
tobacco pipes.

                         PENN
          An honour to meet you again, Mr.
          Harrington. And you, Mr. Neville.
          I see you have not lost your genius
          for mockery, Sir.
                         (MORE)

PENN (CONT'D)
Some months ago, you had published
a letter supposedly from Machiavel
crying his book *The Prince* was but
a satire of tyrants. Yet it was
dated April 1, 1537! The Fool's Day
of April. It didst not escape me.

NEVILLE
Well done, Billy. Thy eye is as
sharp as Cromwell's sword. Ye shall
do well. What is this news I hear,
that you are planning democratic
things for America? You shall have
success, for sure - they are all
Roundheads over there.

PENN
Marry, we are planning great
things, Mr. Neville. I and my
congregation, the Society of
Friends. Hyde didst all he could to
ensure religious liberty be not
honoured in this country. And even
though the Lord Chancellor is now
deposed and dead, harassment
continues. We Quakers have no
choice but to seek freedom
elsewhere. We have chosen America
as our new home and will be
establishing settlements there most
jointly.

HARRINGTON
America? 'Twere always my dream to
go thither. To see this astonishing
waterfall the Franciscan monk
Hannepin talks about. Betwixt some
giant lakes called Ontario and
Erie, I believe. It pours so much
water the universe does not afford
a parallel. It makes the cathedrals
and castles of Europe simply
children's playhouses. Whither are
you planning to settle?

PENN
Further south of that territory,
Sir. We are hoping to purchase the
province of West Jersey, not far
from New York.
(MORE)

PENN (CONT'D)
I have approached the King about
settling his debts with my late
father by granting me a charter for
land extending some forty-five
thousand square miles west of New
Jersey and north of Maryland. I am
planning to call it Sylvania.

HARRINGTON
"Sylvania." That is the Latin for
"forests" is it not?

PENN
Yes, Sir. But the King thinks
better it reflect his deep respect
for the Admiral. What he will name
it, he hath not decided.

NEVILLE
And what of its government,
William?

PENN
This is why I have come, Sir. To
pay my utmost respect to thee, Mr.
Harrington. I intend to draft a
frame of government for this colony
based on *Oceana*'s ideas. Do you
remember how you described those
ideas that night at the Rota? That
we must establish a democracy where
liberty of conscience is its own
state? That a free mind, a free
speech and a free country might not
but go together? Sylvania's
constitution shall protect liberty
of conscience and the free right of
religion.

HARRINGTON
Hardy words spoken yet ne'r
realised, at least not in England.
I went to prison and *Oceana* went
with me. Henry, too, went to prison
a year after, and from what Pepys
tells me, so have you. *Oceana*'s
utopia is only a jail cell.

NEVILLE
My God! We are having a reunion
here! Harrington, Neville, Penn. We
just need old Barebones to make it
complete. It should become an
annual event.
(MORE)

                    NEVILLE (CONT'D)
          Instead of the Rota Club, we shall
          bid it the Political Prisoners'
          Club!

                    PENN
          What befell, Mr. Harrington? Who
          betrayed you?

                    ANNE
          Lady Ashton says ne'r to speak more
          of it. And she be right. The clever
          thing now is to just stay alive.
          James was reduced to a skeleton on
          St. Nicholas Island. Yet at least
          he walked out alive. Better than
          executed like Henry Vane at Tower
          Hill. Or having his head stuck up
          on a pole like Oliver Cromwell.
          Even his daughter, Lady Claypole,
          that distinguished woman to whom
          James once appealed for help, had
          her dead body ripped from its
          burial spot in the Abbey and placed
          in a common pit with twenty others.
          Lady Ashton feels it is for James'
          protection he keep silent about
          forms of government and compose no
          inquiry about his betrayal. She is
          keeping the manuscript he was
          writing in his library the day of
          his arrest. She is compiling a
          collection of his papers but lets
          none see them, not even James.
          Elizabeth is not wrong. My husband
          shall be hurt no more nor our lives
          more shattered.

                    NEVILLE
          Lady Ashton has reason. We shall
          never know for sure, Billy, who
          betrayed James since nought can be
          proved. Hyde operated with many
          spies. Always did, even when in
          exile with the late King. But I
          have my suspicions.

                    HARRINGTON
          Denbigh says we shall never know.

          Neville looks at Harrington and shakes his head.

                    NEVILLE
          Denbigh? James, you trust too much!
          He was a false fellow to everybody.
                    (MORE)

NEVILLE (CONT'D)

The old Pope in Rome saw Denbigh's
deviousness. He betrayed Charles
and after, his own father. Then he
traitored again. Cromwell and
Joyce felt he was switching back to
the royalist side and delaying
things at Holmby which is why they
kidnapped Charles and put him under
the army's charge. I was aye
surprised how much Denbigh knew
that morrow about your arrest. Yet
what may I say? The man hath been
married four times. Even his wives
could not bear him. He has found
his proper home in the House of
Lords.

HARRINGTON

Now be not the time for me to judge
anyone, so close to mine end. There
are days when the palsy leaves my
face without feeling and the gout
sets my feet on fire. And other
days whenst my mind is barely sane.
Yet Anne, you are here to comfort
me. As well as you, Henry. You
never forsooke me. I am blessed and
content. On politics I say no more
but this one thing. Even though
mine memory is being taken away,
would I recall that last night upon
our Coffee Club, I told you,
William Penn, if this age fails me,
the next will do me justice. I set
my sight on a wonderous objective -
building an immortal republic. Yet
my ambition was perhaps too high,
too impractical. Perfection is in
God only, not in the things He has
created. I tried to change
traditional notions but fell short.
Yet what Machiavel saith cannot
stand. We need ideals as much as
facts. Man has reason, yes, but
also fantasy. Get thee to America,
young William. In *Oceana*, I
predicted our colonies there are
yet babes who suckle their Mother's
breast. When they come of age, they
will wean themselves and need no
longer imperialist England. America
must stand for hope. My eternal
prayer will be it not disappoint.
Let not *Oceana* be forgotten there.

(MORE)

HARRINGTON (CONT'D)
                Ensure its orders are true. A
                republic born crooked will never be
                straight. Show future ages there is
                at least one place in this heavy,
                heavy world where religious
                toleration and democracy can be
                found. Compose a constitution that
                ends despotism and corruption. See
                to it that its checks are firm
                enough to prevent even the most
                dangerous demagogue from misusing
                his powers. Knowing this, I shall
                die satisfied my life was not in
                vain.

Pause.

"The *Oceana* is the only valuable model of a commonwealth,
that has yet been offered to the public." David Hume, British
philosopher, 1777

Harrington's *Oceana* is a "specimen of that kind of reading
which produced the American constitutions." John Adams,
Second President of the United States, 1787

"Harrington was the greatest of political theorists." Isaac
Disraeli, father of Benjamin Disraeli, British Prime
Minister, 1841

Harrington's ideas constituted "a notable anticipation of the
materialist conception of history elaborated by Marx and
Engels." Eduard Bernstein, German socialist, 1895

"Harrington's innovative and engaging ideas deserve to be
better known, not the least as they have particular relevance
in the current turbulent political climate." Rachel
Hammersley, Newcastle University

Pause.

In 1664, Basil Fielding, the Earl of Denbigh, was created a
Baron.

In 1666, Edward Hyde was impeached by the House of Commons
for violations of *Habeas Corpus* and forced into exile in
France.

In 1681, Henry Neville published *Plato Redivivus* which
applied Harrington's model to the restoration of monarchy in
England.

Also in 1681, William Penn was granted a charter from King
Charles II for a large tract of land in America.

Penn drew up its first constitution incorporating many of Harrington's ideas. The King named this new colony Pennsylvania.

In 1700, Harrington's manuscript *A System of Politics* was finally published.

Pause.

James Harrington died on September 7, 1677. He is buried in St. Margaret's Church, beside the grave of Sir Walter Raleigh.

INT. BBC TELEVISION STUDIO, LONDON - SAME EVENING

The interview with George Orwell has finished.

> INTERVIEWER
> That concludes our interview, Mr. Orwell. Thanks again.

Orwell nods and puts out his cigarette. He begins coughing once more. He rises and leaves the studio. The Interviewer starts gathering her papers and is preparing to depart.

> TELEVISION DIRECTOR (V.O.)
> Ok. Not too bad but I thought George said we shouldn't be long. What was all that about this bloody fellow Harrington? Nobody knows anything of him or his damn book. And this thing about equality of property and wealth? That's communism. Won't do his sales any good. And for God's sake! Let's not get the BBC started about electing a second house of Parliament. All power must remain with the House of Commons. Don't make our politics more complicated than they are. As for good laws, it's strong leaders that make us safe. We just went through a war to prove that point. All right. We'll go over this tomorrow to see what we can use. But there will be nothing about Harrington or his *Oceana*.

Camera zeros in on the poster of Big Brother.

FADE TO BLACK

THE END.

THE END.

AFTERWORD

By Gary W. O'Brien

In a BBC interview, George Orwell recounts the story of James Harrington, a seventeenth century advocate of democracy, who inspired him to write "1984".

My screenplay's logline is fictional. Orwell never gave such an interview recounting Harrington's story and scholarly opinion is that there no conscious link between his utopia and *1984*. Yet, as noted by the screenplay's Interviewer, it seems more than a coincidence that Orwell called his dystopia "Oceania" while Harrington called his utopia "Oceana".

Orwell had some knowledge of Harrington, as his review of the Margaret James article in the book *The English Revolution 1640, Three Essay*[i], shows. Orwell described James' essay as "the most interesting" and states "a parallel undoubtedly exists" between the seventeenth century "and the one we are in now". In her essay, James characterizes Harrington as "a man of great intellect", an "English gentlemen, traveller and observer, who in his Oceana (published 1656) tried to analyse the reasons for strength and weaknesses in government, and in particular to discover what was happening and why in revolutionary England."[ii] James cites H.F. Russell Smith's seminal work *Harrington and his Oceana* published in 1914. If Orwell had followed up by reading Russell Smith, he would have seen his footnote stating "The life of Harrington by Toland, prefixed to his collection of Harrington's works, was compiled chiefly from material supplied by the Lady Ashton, his eldest sister."[iii] So, it is possible that Orwell was aware of the details of Harrington's story.

There are many other fictional aspects of the screenplay. For example, Caroline Roberts in *Two English Republican Tracts* states that Henry Neville only left England to go to Italy in 1641 when he came of age.[iv] Edward Chaney, however, speculates that Henry may have been in Rome with James in 1636. Chaney says that in January of that year Harrington dined at the Jesuit-run English College with James Zouche and perhaps Henry Neville or his brother Richard. Chaney writes there was "something like a travel craze and it was not unusual to break off one's studies to go abroad in this period. The fact that Henry's older brother, Richard, was abroad and probably in Italy in 1636 make it possible he is the *Pilgrim-Book*'s 'D. Nevellus'. At the very least this would provide us our earliest reference to a personal link between the two classical republicans...."[v]

Likewise, there is no evidence William Penn accompanied Samuel Pepys to a meeting of the Rota on February 20, 1660, although Penn was Pepys' nextdoor neighbour, and Pepys, who was a paid-up member of the club, did make an entry in his *Diary* about attending with a friend what was to be its last meeting.[vi] It is doubtful if Penn ever met Harrington at all, although he may have read *Oceana* while studying at Oxford.[vii]

Still, there is much in the screenplay that is true. For example, Harrington's meeting with Pope Urban VIII at Candlemass; Harrington attending to King Charles I at Holdenby House; the arrest of Charles by Cornet Joyce which Harrington witnessed; Harrington being on the scaffold when the King was beheaded[viii]; *Oceana* being stolen at the printer and Harrington going to see Lady Claypole requesting she prevail upon her father to restore the confiscated material; Neville presenting a *Humble Petition of Divers Well Affected Persons* to the House of Commons on July 6, 1659, and the response of the House thanking him; the meetings of the Rota Club in Westminster beginning in the fall of 1659; Harrington's arrest in November 1661 and his imprisonment in the Tower and then on St. Nicholas Island; and tragically, Harrington's addiction to guaiacum which brought on delusions his perspiration turned into flies.

Also true is Harrington's influence on colonial America. Russell Smith writes that in 1676, one year after the fictional meeting on Birdcage Walk between Penn, Neville, James and Anne, a frame of government for Pennsylvania was drawn up "probably by Penn himself, in which a combination of democracy and toleration was attempted. The constitution is interesting especially for three of its provisions, all of which may be paralleled from, if they were not suggested by, Harrington's writings".[ix]

The Fifth Monarchist Praisegod Barebones was a real person as was Anne Darrell, Lady Ashton, Basil Fielding (the Earl of Denbigh), the Earl of Carnwath, Sir George Carteret, Pastor Greene, Cornet George Joyce, Lady Claypole and her daughter Martha, Samuel Gott, Matthew Wren, Lord Lauderdale, the Earl of Bath, and of course, Edward Hyde, Earl of Clarendon and Lord Chancellor, one of the darker figures of English history.

This is hardly an original screenplay. Much of the language is taken from Harrington's and Neville's own writings. The Lauderdale interview was written by Harrington himself and can be found in the Toland collection. The script for Harrington's meeting with Lady Claypole comes mostly from Toland. The exchange between Charles and Cornet Joyce is taken from J.G. Muddiman's *Trial of King Charles I*. Major elements of the dialogue elsewhere originates from material listed in the bibliography below.

There were two general purposes for writing the screenplay. The first is obvious: the character of Harrington and his story are too intriguing not to be brought to life. Though much is imagined, it is hoped the flavour of the language of seventeenth century England has to some extent been successfully captured.

Secondly, I wanted to draw attention to the importance of Harrington's politics to issues facing many parliaments and legislatures today. As someone who worked professionally in a parliament his entire career, what attracted me to Harrington was his belief in bicameralism, that is, a legislature composed of two separate houses. Harrington felt the question of bicameralism was the most important question in politics. In *Oceana*, he writes: "There is not a more noble or useful question in the politics than that which is started by Machiavel: whether means were to be found whereby the enmity that was between the senate and the people of Rome might have been removed. Nor is there any other in which we, or the present occasion, are so much concerned, particularly in relation unto this author; for as much as, his judgment in the determination of the question standing, our commonwealth falleth."[x] His elation in the screenplay when he discovers how Neville's two silly girls divided Jessy's cake, showing him how a bicameral legislature can best share their powers, bears this out.

Harrington was adamant that democratic institutions go beyond power relations and instead seek "a Union of the Interests of the whole Nation in the Government." Without providing a precise definition, Harrington felt this union of interests differed from private reason, which "is the interest of a private man" or the reason of the state "which is the interest …of the rulers, that is to say of the prince, the nobility, or of the people." The common interest was "the interest of mankind or of the whole." Such a universal interest could only be found through a new parliamentary system in which the legislative was of greater importance than the executive and where authority was a leading government principle.[xi]

Harrington vigorously opposed Hobbesian unicameralism[xii], and more specifically the Rump, the new symbol of England's democracy. He saw the Rump as anarchial, driven by passion, fortune and private interests, without "any covenants, conditions, or orders whatsoever." It rested only on power. It had destroyed executive power and one half of legislative power, leaving it the only legal authority. Its January 4, 1649 declaration – "that the people of England, are under God, the original of all just power; that the Commons of England, by and representing the people, have the supreme power in this realm" – made no mention of authority. Such a foundation could only lead to the workways of corruption. Harrington would not have disagreed with Cromwell's assessment that the rumpers were "drunkards" and "whoremasters", nor with the traditional historical view that "by 1653 they had become intolerably oligarchical, dilatory and corrupt."[xiii]

Harrington argued for an upper house architecture which was democratic and effective, on which would do away with the distinction between power and authority, making Cicero's puzzle - "why does the upper house have authority even when the lower house is granted the power of decision?"[xiv] – extraneous. But his model could not be achieved by parliamentary reform alone. James's brilliance was that he saw the functioning of parliament not as the output of an independent institution but one dependent upon a number of other variables within the political system, namely the state of societal conditions; the electoral system; the party system; political socialization; and above all else, constitutional prescriptions. He could not emphasize more the importance of holding constitutional discussions.

One of Harrington's principal attacks was on the formation of political factions. He anticipated the comment made over three hundred years later by Professor Vernon Bogdanor who wrote "the dominance of party politics in modern democracies" has meant that "the practice of bicameralism bears very little relation to the theory."[xv] Harrington advocated that political parties be discouraged through a complicated legislative voting system and other measures. As parliamentary reformists search for alternatives to the problems of representative institutions, unicameralism, party government, executive dominance, gridlock and adversarial debate, Harrington seems very relevant.

More recently, Maxwell Cameron has observed that "political institutions...are failing to respond to many of the biggest collectivist challenges of our times...(T)o exert a positive influence, institutions require people with the will and skill to serve the common good...."[xvi] For those who feel the authoritarian character of institutions must become more important with a greater stress on ethics and a lessening of party dominance within parliamentary life, *Oceana* may be instructive on how power and ethics can be combined within a bicameral system.

I would like to thank Professors Glenn Burgess (University of Hull), Rachel Hammersley (Newcastle University), and Edward Chaney (University College London) for their helpful suggestions and encouragement, and to my family - Colette, Kevin and Emilie - and my sister Cheryl, for their support.

GARY W. O'BRIEN was born in 1951 in Toronto and served as Clerk of the Senate of Canada and Clerk of the Parliaments from 2009-2015. He holds a Ph.D. in political science from Carleton University, Ottawa and has published articles in the *Canadian Journal of Political Science*, *Ontario History*, the *Canadian Parliamentary Review* and *The Table*. He is the author of *Oswald's Politics* (Trafford Publishing, 2010). He can be reached at garyobrien@sympatico.ca.

Endnotes

[i] Orwell, George, "Review of The English Revolution: 1640" in George Orwell, Peter Davison, Timothy Garton Ash, *Orwell and Politics* (Penguin Modern Classics).

[ii] Margaret James, "Contemporary Materialist Interpretations in the English Revolution" in Christopher Hill (ed.), *The English Revolution, Three Essays* (London: Lawrence and Wishart, 1940), p. 85.

[iii] H.F. Russell Smith, *Harrington and His Oceana: A Study of a 17th Century Utopia and Its Influence in America* (New York: Octagon Books, 1971), p.3.

[iv] Caroline A. Robbins (ed.), *Two English Republican Tracts* (Cambridge: Cambridge University Press, 1969), p. 5

[v] Edward Chaney, *The Grand Tour and the Great Rebellion: Richard Lassells and "The Voyage of Italy" in the Seventeenth Century* (Geneva: Centro Interuniversitario di Ricerche sul Viaggio in Italia), p. 286

[vi] Michael Downs, *James Harrington* (Twayne Publishers, 1977), p. 130.

[vii] Russell Smith, *op.cit.*, p. 167.

[viii] It is doubtful, however, if it was Charles who encouraged Harrington to write *Oceana*. More likely it was some "officers" of the newly created Lord Protector. See Paul Rahe, *Against Throne and Altar: Machiavelli and Political Theory under the English Republic* (Cambridge: Cambridge University Press, 2008), pp. 321-22.

[ix] *Ibid.*, p. 162.

[x] James Harrington, *The Commonwealth of Oceana and A System of Politics*, edited by J.G.A. Pocock (Cambridge: Cambridge University Press, 1992), p. 155.

xi See *The Humble Petition of Divers Well Affected Persons*, July 6, 1659; and *Oceana* (Pocock), p. 21. Charles Blitzer writes: "...the parliament of Oceana possesses the authority to choose the members of the executive branch of government, to supervise their activities...". *An Immortal Commonwealth: The Political Thought of James Harrington* (Archon Books, 1970), p. 235.

xii In *Leviathan*, Hobbes writes "The only way to erect such a Common Power...is, to conferre all their power and strength upon one Man, or upon one Assembly of men, that may reduce all their Wills, by plurality of voices, unto one Will...." Thomas Hobbes, *Leviathan*, edited by C.B. Macpherson (Pelican Classics, 1968), p. 227.

xiii Blair Worden, *The Rump Parliament 1648-1653* (Cambridge: Cambridge University Press, 1974), pp. 336, 384.

xiv See Jeanette Money and George Tsebelis, "Cicero's Puzzle: Upper House Power in Comparative Perspective", *International Political Science Review*, 1992, Vol. 13, No. 1., pp. 25-26.

xv Vernon Bogdanor, *Politics and the Constitution: Essays on British Government* (Dartmouth Publishing, 1996), p. 258.

xvi Maxwell A. Cameron, *Political Institutions and Political Wisdom: Between Rules and Practices* (Oxford: Oxford University Press, 2018), Introduction.

Bibliography

Aubrey, John, *Brief Lives* (Oxford: Oxford University Press, 2015).

Ashley, Maurice, *John Wildman: Plotter and Postmaster* (New Haven, Yale University Press, 1947).

Blitzer, Charles, *An Immortal Commonwealth: The Political Thought of James Harrington* (Archon Books, 1970).

Braddick, Michael J., *The Oxford Handbook of the English Revolution* (Oxford: Oxford University Press, 2015).

Burgess, Glenn, "Repacifying the polity: the responses of Hobbes and Harrington to the crisis of the common law" in Gentles, Ian, John Morrill and Blair Worden (eds.), *Soldiers, Writers and Statesmen of the English Revolution* (Cambridge: Cambridge University Press, 1998).

Burton, Thomas, *Diary of Thomas Burton, esq., Member in the Parliaments of Oliver and Richard Cromwell* (Select Scholar, Wentworth Press).

Cameron, Maxwell A., *Political Institutions and Political Wisdom: Between Rules and Practices* (Oxford: Oxford University Press, 2018).

Capp, Bernard, *The Fifth Monarchy Men: A Study in Seventeenth Century English Millenarianism* (Faber and Faber).

Carlton, Charles, *Charles I: The Personal Monarch* (London: Routledge and Kegan Paul, 1983).

Downs, Michael, *James Harrington* (Twayne Publishers, 1977).

Edwards, Graham, *The Last Days of Charles I* (Gloucestershire: Sutton Publishing, 1999).

Foster, Elizabeth Read, *The House of Lords 1603-1649* (Chapel Hill and London: The University of North Carolina Press, 1983).

Fink, Zera S., *The Classical Republicans: An Essay on the Recovery of a Pattern of Thought in Seventeenth-Century England* (Eugene, Oregon: Resource Publications, 2011, second edition).

Hammersley, Rachel, *James Harrington: An Intellectual Biography* (Oxford: Oxford University Press, 2019).

Harrington, James, *The Oceana of James Harrington, Esq. and His Other Works, with an account of his life by John Toland Prefix'd* (Dublin: Riley, Smith and Bruce, 1737).

Harrington, James, *The Commonwealth of Oceana and A System of Politics*, edited by J.G.A. Pocock (Cambridge: Cambridge University Press, 1992).

Herbert, Thomas, *Memoirs of the Two Last Years of the Reign of King Charles* 1 (London: W. Bulmer, 1813).

Hobbes, Thomas, *Leviathan*, edited by C.B. Macpherson (Pelican Classics, 1968).

Hyde, Edward, Earl of Clarendon, *The History of the Rebellion*, edited by Paul Seaward (Oxford: Oxford World Classics, 2009).

James, Margaret, "Contemporary Materialist Interpretations in the English Revolution" in Christopher Hill (ed.), *The English Revolution, Three Essays* (London: Lawrence and Wishart, 1940).

Khouri, Nadia, "Reaction and Nihilism: The Political Genealogy of Orwell's 1984", *Science Fiction Studies*, 12 (1985), pp. 136-47.

Mahlberg, Gaby, *Henry Neville and the English Republican culture in the seventeenth century: Dreaming of Another Game* (Manchester and New York: Manchester University Press, 2009).

Mayers, Ruth E., *1659: The Crisis of the Commonwealth* (The Royal Historical Society, The Boydell Press, 2004).

Money, Jeanette and George Tsebelis, "Cicero's Puzzle: Upper House Power in Comparative Perspective", *International Political Science Review*, 1992, Vol. 13, No. 1., 25-43.

Muddiman, J.G., *Trial of King Charles I* (Glasgow and Edinburgh: William Hodge and Co. Ltd.).

Murphy, Andrew R., *The Political Writings of William Penn* (Indianapolis: Liberty Fund, 2002).

Neville, Henry, *The Humble Petition of Divers Well Affected Persons,* Presented to the House of Commons, July 6, 1659.

Neville, Henry, *The Parliament of Ladies...and The Isle of Pines,* edited by Thomas Hollis (1768).

Neville, Henry, *Plato Redivivus; or, A Dialogue Concerning Government,* Second Edition, 1681 (Dodo Press).

O'Brien, Gary William, "The Validity of Bicameralism: The Views of Harrington and Bentham", Paper presented at the Annual Meeting of the Canadian Political Science Association, June 2019.

Orwell, George, *George Orwell's 1984* (Civitas Library Classics).

Orwell, George, "Review of The English Revolution: 1640" in George Orwell, Peter Davison, Timothy Garton Ash, *Orwell and Politics* (Penguin Modern Classics).

Pepys, Samuel, *The Diary of Samuel Pepys,* Volume 1 (London: George Bell and Sons, 1893).

Pocock, J.G.A., "Machiavelli, Harrington and English Political Ideology", *William and Mary Quarterly,* Vol. 22, No. 4, 1965.

Pocock, J.G. A., "James Harrington and the Good Old Cause", *Journal of British Studies*, Vol. 10, No. 1, 1970.

Rahe, Paul, *Against Throne and Altar: Machiavelli and Political Theory under the English Republic* (Cambridge: Cambridge University Press, 2008).

Robbins, Caroline A., *The Eighteenth Century Commonwealthman* (Indianapolis: Liberty Fund, 1987).

Robbins, Caroline A. (ed.)., *Two English Republican Tracts* (Cambridge: Cambridge University Press, 1969).

Scott, Jonathan, "The rapture of motion: James Harrington's republicanism" in Phillipson, Nicholas and Quentin Skinner, *Political Discourse in Early Modern Britain (*Cambridge: Cambridge University Press, 1993).

Shklar, Judith, "Ideology Hunting: The Case of James Harrington", *American Political Science Review*, 53 (September 1959).

Smith, H.F. Russell, *Harrington and His Oceana*: *A Study of a 17th Century Utopia and Its Influence in America* (New York: Octagon Books, 1971).

Strauss, Leo, *What is Political Philosophy? And Other Studies* (Westport, Conn.: Greenwood Press, 1973).

Tuck, Richard, *Philosophy and Government 1572-1651* (Cambridge: Cambridge University Press, 1993).

Underdown, David, "The Harringtonian Moment", *Journal of British Studies*, Vol. 18, No. 2, Spring, 1979.

Wood, Anthony, *Athenea Oxonienses*, Volume 3 (London: 1817).

Zagorin, Parez, *A History of Political Thought in the English Revolution* (London: Routledge and Kegan Paul, 1954).